As a wife, mother and grandmother, Linda has traveled a path of an incredible spiritual awakening. Apart from being a certified Holistic Health Counselor, Metaphysical Practitioner and self-published, Linda is known as a Spiritual teacher and Mystic Energy Healer for over a decade. In 2017, she began her journey of channeling. An avid reader and lover of the unseen world, the discovery of how her personal totem animals have guided her life led to this book. Meeting her Dragon Spirit Guide, she calls Violet was a gift.

For my grandchildren:

Hunter, Hudson, Jameson, Franco, Salvatore, Luciana, Bradley, Nev and Baby Girl Landano, as well as all the Children of the World…

May you be Blessed to Stay in Wonder, Joy and Happiness!

Linda Amato

A Key to the Unseen World

A Discovery of Self

Austin Macauley Publishers

LONDON • CAMBRIDGE • NEW YORK • SHARJAH

Ordering Information
Quantity sales: Special discounts are available on quantity purchases by corporations, associations, and others. For details, contact the publisher at the address below.

Publisher's Cataloging-in-Publication data
Amato, Linda
A Key to the Unseen World

ISBN 9781647504601 (Paperback)
ISBN 9781647504595 (Hardback)
ISBN9781647504618 (ePub e-book)

Library of Congress Control Number: 2022902125

www.austinmacauley.com/us

First Published 2023
Austin Macauley Publishers LLC
40 Wall Street, 33rd Floor, Suite 3302
New York, NY 10005
USA

mail-usa@austinmacauley.com
+1 (646) 5125767

Personally, IAM aware I have been guided by Spirit to read certain books, attend many workshops, summits and be inspired by teachers who have come into my life! I treasure their teachings ….

As well as my husband and children!

For all of us our strongest teachers are those closest to us to awaken to that which is part of our lesson plan.

"IAM GRATEFUL BEYOND ALL MEASURE OF BELIEF TO THE SPIRITUAL TEACHERS OF THE WORLD – THE ALCHEMISTS!"

I send light and love to Julee Love for connecting me to Violet, My Dragon Spirit Guide

"Archangel Metatron I thank you for showing me clear communication with my guides and to be able to trust their wisdom…" – Alphedia Arara

"May all that I gaze upon be blessed…" – Stephanie Lodge

"Elemental Beings, You have served us. Now it is our turn, we, the IAM Race, to serve you, to demand your Resurrection…" – Mother Akasha's Radiant Rose Academy

Part One

Chapters 1 to 17…is the journey of Kali Lunar growing up, becoming a wife and mother connected to the unseen world in many ways. The support, guidance, and insight from Totem Spirit Animals and Guides, allowed Kali to thrive in the depths of despair…

Part Two

Day 1 to Day 222…Kali's world opens to the magnificent communication from Violet, her Dragon Spirit Guide of the unseen world…

The conclusion of this discovery of self-empowers Kali to share her beliefs, story, and collaboration with the world of Spirit today as she knows of its power to help humanity…

Part One
The Essence of Being Human

Introduction

In this story that all of humanity travels through, you will meet the many voices of guidance that await humanity daily. It is a story with a map and key of ancient wisdom that configures our life through the points of the journey taken. We are all supported by different energies at different points on our personal paths that are unseen. Kali discovers the ability to communicate with the unseen world as she reflects on the many challenges and chaos she has experienced. In the back of her mind, there was always an inner belief that she never felt she was alone.

Mywolf is a mystical figure in the mind of Kali. In reality, he is a spirit guide/totem animal for her. They have traveled lifetimes together. The veil is thin from one dimension to another, as Kali knows of never feeling alone. Her lifetime struggles are part of the plan to discover who she is. It is a journey and path many do not follow. Her being aware is a gift Mywolf gave to her. Life is to awaken to self. To enjoy is to discover a love for self. Kali senses one is to realize there is truth, in life and illusion.

Can it be, Kali ponders, everyone is an alien from another planet? Nothing is as it looks to be.

These memories stir her soul. To discover where she has been. To recognize where she is going. Surrounded by this inner belief, she is never alone. Kali is eager to discover those that are traveling alongside her. She has an ache to experience everything which can set her free from humanity's beliefs.

Mywolf has been guiding her forward in life for as long as he can remember. It is the ability she has within, which has made it possible. Her belief to live out of the box has created doors to open in her mind. Kali is a mystical creature herself from a world full of magic and love. It is in her soul to uncover teachings to raise her vibration and humanity's. Life has granted her to awaken to incredible alternatives of study. Despair, drama, crisis, and fear engulfed her young. To experience a life filled with joy guides her. Kali's biggest question this life has always been to understand why others are mean to one another and abusive. She has struggled with this, and her gift to love humanity is the result.

Mywolf has waited lifetimes to empower Kali into the realm of other dimensions. A discovery of self is the hardest for humans to acknowledge, Mywolf imagined. In this story, Kali travels the journey of her map through identification, unconditional love, awakening, and her spirituality to include all she had forgotten from her past lifetimes.

Kali does not differ from another woman that struggles daily with the responsibilities of their lives. Most women accept motherhood is the joy of their lives, and guilt is the gift given to them instead. This guilt stems from a society that views and declares that women need to do it all. However, it is only the men in this human undertaking that struggle with the fear they are the ones that must do it all. This is where the battle begins. In the past, women stayed home to raise the children and take care of the house while their husbands went to work. Today, women work right alongside men. It generates guilt from this want to work for women today.

Mywolf is a totem animal/spirit guide for Kali for all her lifetimes. It is this life experience where she desires to experience him and let him lead her further on her journey. This is Mywolf's story, and he will explain it as only he can because he knows Kali best of all. There is a world humanity has forgotten that is not similar to this earthly one, but yet it is right alongside traveling everyone's life experience with them. This is the world of dimensions, faeries, elementals, totem animals, Spirit Guides, Angels, Ascended Masters, Saints, and our loved ones that have transitioned. Life is eternal, and the truth is that no one dies.

Mywolf reflects on humanity, knowing there comes a time in life where one desires a change, a growth, or just to remember that there is more in life. There has to be more! The more which humans search for is *"the all that is."* To find *"the all that is"* leads a human to an alternative belief that may be difficult for others to comprehend. It is Kali's journey into the realm of *"the all that is"* that opens the doors for her discovery of self with the guidance and support of Mywolf.

Humans have many beliefs that stem from their societal thoughts. Mywolf knows it matters not, your age, for age is a human belief. The keys of discovery are within and will be for you to seek.

- It matters not, your generational beliefs, because they are all from a society of humans.
- It matters not, what you see because there is more to see that is possible.
- It matters not, who you assume you are as a human because you are a spiritual being living as a human.
- It matters not, your religion, for this, too, is a human experience.
- What matters is that you awaken to knowing you are a human being of light and love.

Mywolf will share with you the transformation of this spiritual awakening from a human experience that asked for more because she identified in the essence of her being that there had to be more to this life. The saying is, *"If you ask, you shall receive."* Kali asked and what unfolded for her as the answer is a life of joy, happiness, creativity, balance, and wholeness. To witness that anything is possible. That there is a reason for everything in life because there are no mistakes, only lessons we can learn from.

Kali is brilliant! Confident, full of joy, and inner peace. No one would suspect she has struggled through abuse, abandonment, addiction, and at one time, fear filled her. It began when Mywolf sent many other spirit guides/totem animals to comfort her. She suspected they had a purpose as they offered her happiness within, she could not explain. It became her ability to collect these different totem animals, which put a smile on her face and joy in her heart. She became attached to them. Another traumatic experience arrived and threatened her. A new totem animal then arrives by Mywolf to offer her clarity and insight.

Kali always maintained a connection with a divine intelligence; God, Angels, Saints, and Ascended Masters. There surfaced a time, after a meditation where she identified with her own inner vision, the Master Healer, Jesus the Christ. She sensed Him walking alongside her daily. It comforted her to pray and reach out to angels and archangels. Her favorite Archangels being Michael, Raphael, Uriel, Gabrielle, and Metatron. Years ago, she had connected to the Blessed Mother Mary by the pure understanding she is the Mother of every woman and child. It comforted her to talk to Blessed Mother Mary through prayer and thank her for her guidance and protection.

Kali is a dreamer, and her dreams embraced love and helping others. She enjoyed living life. People may even refer to her as an elemental.

A reader as well, she gravitated to books on royalty, history, Arthur and the Knights of the Round Table, Merlin, esoteric, metaphysical, angels, aromatherapy, prayer, and biography. Any type of science fiction movies filled her with an inner knowing that there is more to life. Her simplicity to life enabled her to go with the flow. She never questioned, nor did she act confrontational. Human behavior intrigued her. Why people spoke and acted as they did. The depths of her thoughts always took her to want to discover as much as possible concerning life. This is a joined creation story of Mywolf and Kali Lunar. A discovery of the self!

Chapter One
Into the Woods

Kali hiked into the woods. Surrounded by the elegance of Mother Nature. A brisk morning that nourished her soul as she held on to the walking sticks for balance. Her heart jumped into her chest as she marveled at this property, this forest, her woods. All 165 acres to discover as often as she chose filled her with excitement. She could hear the waterfall, but could not see it, so she stopped to get her bearings.

Turning to the right toward the rocky path, Kali tried to balance herself. The sound of the water on the rocks became louder as she stopped and caught her breath! Right before her eyes, she saw the waterfall. She loved the entranceway to the waterfall, a steep slope going downwards with arched trees that seemed to bow to her as she walked. Trees surrounded her path, and since coming into the forest, Kali noticed the trees in her life daily. She understood them as guardians for the people who shared the planet with humanity. Mywolf seemed aware of the deep respect and love that Kali held in her heart for Mother Nature as he walked alongside her to the waterfall.

A smile crossed her lips as she took in the vision of Mother Nature that surrounded her. Kali saw the small bench she had placed right by the waterfall to meditate. She sat, closed her eyes, took a deep breath in, and calmed her heart. Sitting straight with her hands on her knees, she relaxed. She drifted into the calmest of places filled with her totem animals, and her present one, the wolf she had named Mywolf. Daily, she has been learning from him. Kali was amazed at the insight she received from the totem animals throughout her life.

Understanding always that there is a reason for everything, she now found herself in need of this spot on the planet. The energy, charm, calmness, and magical pull it owned is undeniable. The energy lifted her soul as she smelled the air and listened to the song of the birds. Even the movement of the trees and wildflowers delighted her as nourishment. There was a time she did not comprehend what she needed to discover; however, today, Kali perceived it had to be to find out who she is in the way of helping humanity.

Mywolf gave Kali the image everyone is given at birth with passion and purpose to discover as their reason for being. The many gifts that humans are born with but ignore amazed Mywolf.

There is a plan, a path, a journey to achieve Kali pondered. It all added up to the years of change that, once started, will not end. A calling that filled her mind, body, and soul every wakening moment. The teachers, authors, books, classes, and retreats she needed to breathe in. Kali had now discovered something that delighted her senses, the world of the unknown beings, elementals, and the faeries!

Now, she perceived she would never be alone. Kali senses a presence, eyes upon her. Giggling to herself, it seemed wonderful to breathe in this air. She heard the rustle of the trees and the smell of earth that surrounded her as she sat with the splashing of the water on the rocks. Praying that when she opened her eyes, she would see a deer or even a bear. Opening her eyes, she took out her Phone and took pictures of this place; she appeared to connect to in a way she had not known possible. There was an energy here of peace and love. That's it; she seemed loved here. Kali realized she belonged here.

She noticed the timing in everything. She seemed ready! Now she desired to sit here daily by the waterfall and enjoy the quiet as she meditated, tasted the air, and breathed in the love. She wondered what would be next.

She took the waterfall in her mind's eye and placed it there for the times she would be away. The energy engulfed her and filled her with joy. She recollected that during guided meditations, it seemed as if this property had appeared for her to walk. She smiled. Kali loved her life!

Mywolf watched as Kali took in the beauty that surrounded her; the movement of the trees, the cool brisk wind, birds chirping in the trees, and the pleasure in knowing of the elements of life as her feet brought up the energy of Gaia into her body. The earth spirit guides, water, spirit guides, fire spirit guides, and the air spirit guides all surrounded her at this very moment. Mywolf knew that Kali sensed the energy but was not ready as of yet to embrace all that will eventually be hers to share.

Chapter Two
The Tribe

Mywolf seated himself in the window of her mind's eye, knowing she was a slow learner and someone who requires the patience of him. His qualities were many, but he savored his ability to be part of a tribe. To be her protector for all these lifetimes ignited bliss. Mywolf appreciated his reliability in knowing what she needed to connect to another dimension. Her new tribe would be the faery, and they would be the ones to guide her to open to channel and raise humanity's vibration.

As part of her world, he supported her choices and let her perceive what he expected of her. The woods seemed vast in life, with many trees, animals, sights, and sounds. It would be easy for her to get lost within herself and not find what to expect of herself. To sit at the waterfall and meditate is a beginning. To reflect into her mind's eyes, the waterfall is the gift of putting herself there when needed. The time will come when she will receive advice to put herself into other dimensions to learn and recognize nothing is as it implies in this world.

Kali was a rare human because she remembered a world called paradise, flowers, green grass, trees, and elementals. At this time, she could not grasp the essence fully, but she knew and sensed in her heart that there was more to life. For her, it seemed a map to follow until the treasures are revealed. She had this inner knowing and sensed that energy played a full part in all life experiences. In her own mind, she always reflected as a child about the Saints, Jesus the Christ, and especially angels and archangels as her friends.

Mywolf was always aware of her connection to the unseen world.

Mywolf lay by the waterfall to nap, to wait. The time was not yet. The time was coming when her vision of herself will be the real vision of who she is. Kali has done her homework, as they say. Still, she has too many responsibilities that drag her away from her path and her journey. Kali needs boundaries. Getting her to stay focused is her greatest challenge. Interruptions take her away from the thoughts in her head, which are needed for her to stay focused, for her to do her part of the work needed for partnership with the faery world.

Humans in her life are in need of her, Mywolf reflects. Kali handles the stops and starts in her life well. She refuses to get overwhelmed because she knows she must live in this world just as she dreams of living in the other world daily.

With all her knowledge, it is now time to uncover the gifts of her wisdom from lifetimes. Her father existed as the greatest of wise men and made choices in his life to empower Kali. His teaching of unconditional love manifested as his greatest gift he bestowed to her. To just love and be kind sounds so simple, but for many, the most difficult feature of being human. She proved herself with him and accepted her reason for being had something to do with him being her father. His sacrifices for her surfaced as his own karma he needed to amend.

It was the father who named her and the first man in her life who taught her of the importance of Mother Nature. To respect and love the land as a young child. Crazy as they say he acted, he gifted her with a love for walking, parks, trees, the beach, swimming, and breathing in the air while the sun warmed her body. For years she survived by this connection. Then she stopped, she became busy with those responsibilities and forgot what nourished her soul. She forgot to get herself outside to breathe in all that is offered.

She trembled at the notion of the sun burning her skin *(this was not her view but a society belief)*. For years, she turned to books to escape the daily life she had manifested. She fell asleep, it seemed to Mywolf, for a long time.

Mywolf had the patience of a saint. He waited. He identified a change was coming. Her responsibilities would change and would leave a void. He would fill the void. Humans, he noticed, cling to things that cannot be changed, especially death. Death found its way into her world just as it finds its way into everyone's life experience. There is no getting away from this word, this action humans label death. Mywolf knew that no one dies ever!

The reality of death is that a human returns home and enters another dimension at the time they have chosen. They need to understand, these humans, that it is only a transition, not death; the soul is eternal, the body is a vehicle. There had been a time when Kali maintained as the rest of humanity and feared death. Mywolf inspired her thoughts to change, and the fear dissipated, and her thoughts ran to acknowledging that life is eternal.

Mywolf closed his eyes to reflect on humanity's beliefs when it came to humanity. They accepted everything they read, saw, or heard. This idea of television, radio, newspapers, and books filled their minds with garbage and lies. Yet, they became attached to this illusion and suffered from it all. Illusion and attachment to the materialistic needs and desires in life seemed to be profound in many of their lives. Many desired to be clueless as to the abilities they owned to determine for themselves. To realize that their body existed as a vehicle, vessel, or temple, and it needed to receive nourishment.

Chapter Three
Alternative Belief

Kali stepped out of the box all of her life from a young age. Found to be extreme in her beliefs, but she never faltered from what she considered important in life. How to be, do, figure out, speak, and act have been her greatest achievements. Mywolf smiled to himself; she had doubt slip in now and then. However, when she admitted something to be her truth, she never faltered. Her young life had been difficult, but yet she learned to empower herself with those around her.

She took her mom's fears and filled herself with the strength to do what her mom chose not to do for an abusive/alcoholic husband. As a child, it appeared ridiculous for her to fear her father; she supposed all he needed was love and someone to talk to and support him. He seemed terrified to her, of life. Mywolf stretched out his paws on the wet grass while the waterfall splashed into the stream, as he basked in the warmth of the sun.

Bracing his head on his paws, he reflected on the journey they have been on together. Her life flew by, so he seemed surprised she awakened when she did. Her responsibilities she handled with force and a knowing filled her entire being. Unconditional love is the foundation for how she raised her children. To be there for them, to listen, respect, and set boundaries for them.

Mywolf remembered that through all the years of making choices, she still cared for her father while raising her children and loving her husband.

Kali closed her mind and eyes to her husband's beliefs, though, and loved him. She always considered it her responsibility for being married to him to love him, accept him, and try to help him. Sometimes though, no one can help another who does not want help. No one can love another unless they let them.

Kali was blind to these qualities of her husband. She gave him love because she saw his fears and felt the pain he held close within his heart. Kali always knew who needed to experience love, and this was a gift she shared.

Mywolf sat up on his back paws so he would not fall asleep and remembered all that the husband provided for Kali and their family. It was everything he needed in life. Most of it was materialistic because money was abundant because of him. He was a powerful man, and although never happy, he got what he wanted when he wanted it. Kali perceived him as brilliant and ready to rescue another if they called on him to do so. A wounded human from many lifetimes of not accepting love or appearing unworthy of love, he never loved Kali because he never loved himself.

Mywolf did not comprehend this ability humans manifested to shut down their hearts completely. He always wondered why they simply did not begin to love themselves first and then project this love outwards to all. It seemed to him that they did the complete opposite. There was no path but the one they chose for themselves. He imagined this stemmed from the separation thing humans enjoyed. In all his lifetimes of journeying along Kali's side, he saw how love may just be the key humans are missing.

Humans threw these three words around as if they meant something, "I love you..." Mywolf identified in his heart love is acceptance, trust, belief, understanding, and allowing another to be themselves in all situations. Love simply is, Mywolf thought. Love is that which is, and it is nothing else. Love is ...

- To talk and listen when another speaks.
- To love is to not judge or criticize anyone.
- To open one's heart to another is to discover their story and support them in their choices.
- To be kind with thought, word and action is true love toward another.
- To not accept the need to defend oneself or to protect oneself from those they love.
- To tell another you see them and you will get them, is an act of love. When one loved themselves, it was then and only then that they can love another.
- To love oneself is to take care of the body, to rest, eat proper foods, and to meditate.

Kali discovered through journaling she loved herself a long time ago. She saw that she was not responsible for making another happy. Her choice was to listen, learn, respect, support, and be there for those she loved when they needed her. A pattern of her belief was to say, "Yes" when others needed her. She embraced a belief she had a choice to, and what she decided on was to choose love in all cases.

Kali traveled a lifetime with spirit totem animals from the dog, monkey, squirrel, pig, swan, deer, frog, seagull, owl, turtle, cat, bear, hawk, horse, octopus, elephant, and now Mywolf. They all had a reason for being with her at a difficult time in her life, depending on what was the directions she needed to travel. Mywolf was her totem for life, and it was Mywolf who summoned the others when needed to help Kali during her life experiences until she was ready to meet Mywolf. The map was the path she traveled with help, always from the unseen world of Spirit; even when she was unaware, she knew in her soul, she was not alone.

These totem animals would appear to Kali in a thought or material form. She would collect aspects of these totems to surround her in her daily life. She was clueless about why she needed to collect pigs, for instance. However, she enjoyed the presence of them daily for years in her life. Whether it be a statue, a picture, a charm, or a piece of jewelry or article that had the totem animal on it. There was a time when she felt Mywolf's presence, but the timing was not right for Mywolf to make himself known to her. To be aware as a human is rare when it comes to the unseen world of protection.

Chapter Four
Totem Animal Spirit Guides

The spirit world and the ability she comprehended when she looked into the meanings of her dreams and totem animals would intrigue Kali. Many traveled alongside her life. Some totem animals stayed with her for years and popped in and out. There was a moment in life where the love of a certain animal comforted Kali. Being drawn to animals for years was a deep secret knowing of hers, that they had a purpose. Kali knew that there had to be a reason for the animals. It was as if she felt their essence in her soul. When she was young, she delighted in their companionship.

It is written that each person has nine different animals that will go with him/her through life, acting as guides. Those with an asterisk are part of Kali's nine.

- ***Dog:** Kali found an attachment to the dog when she was young. She needed unconditional love, and dogs are faithful, loyal, and taught her the basis of unconditional love and allowed her to open her heart even further throughout her life as a totem for her. Dogs have been a strong part of Kali's life to this day. She can communicate with them and understand them.

- ***Monkey:** Offered Kali the ability to change her environment when she was in her twenties. As a totem, it helped her with communication and learning to be adaptable. Personalities and relationships are the hardest, but with the monkey spirit as a totem, Kali adapted to a style of communication that benefited her... See no evil, hear no evil, and speak no evil.

- ***Squirrel:** With the squirrel, it prepared her for challenges and changes coming in her life in her thirties. Kali was playful during this time and very resourceful because of how the squirrel would guide her. She learned what to gather around her to sustain her through coming changes in her life. Knowledge is what she gathered around her to sustain her through the challenges and changes.

- ***Pig:** Being true to herself allowed her spiritual strength to blossom. Prosperity was all around her in her late thirties, and with the pig, she learned to organize and balance her life. To be true to her beliefs. Boundaries, organization, and discovery of her spirituality helped her during this phase of her existence.

- **Swan:** The swan entered her life when the pig was leaving. It was time for appreciating the grace all around her. Grace and rekindling of her love for Mother Nature arrived with the swan as her totem animal. The balance and innocence of life awakened her soul for transformation and dreams coming through. It was when Kali learned to distinguish herself and to go with the flow of life.

- **Deer:** The gift of awareness and learning to trust her instincts by listening to her gut. It was this teaching that allowed her to learn to trust her body for the messages in her life with the deer. Compassion, being kind and gentle on herself and others allowed gracefulness to travel the path with the deer. Not taking everything into her life was learning the depths of trusting herself.

- **Frog:** Learning to adapt and survive, to clean up her body, mind, and soul are the gifts from the frog. Kali grew strong in her forties to face adversity. To accept what was inevitable and what in her mind cannot be changed by her. To survive and seize her potential. With the frog, Kali opened her heart to all during tremendous adversity in her life.

- ***Owl:** In Kali's fifties, wisdom was the main gift from the owl. For her to pay attention to signs, her intuition, messages, to open herself to guidance in her life. To respond to the call of her soul. To never be deceived by the mysteries of life but to choose her freedom. Kali awakened to the depths of the voice of her soul and to nurture it with the owl.

- ***Seagull:** With the seagull, Kali allowed her easy-going nature and creativity to unfold. It was the path of freedom she sought, and with the seagull came versatility and a resourcefulness for her to examine. Kali admired the seagulls flying and their freedom. It was the seagull that taught her to spread her wings and fly.

- ***Turtle:** Slowness was always part of Kali's makeup. Now with the turtle, she learned to retreat to develop patience and take her time. To learn to nurture and nourish herself. In time, she would stick her neck out and make progress toward her goals in life. Turtle helped her develop a way of protecting herself from criticism.

- **Cat:** Detachment was key to the magic in Kali's life. Now in her sixties, there was independence, magic, and mystery that the cat offered to Kali. It was during this time in her life that connected her to love and to detach.

- **Bear:** Kali needed her creativity and to return to what it required, which for her was to set boundaries and stand up for herself. Solitude and healing had been essential in Kali's life when the bear walked into her world. With introspection, courage, and willpower, Kali learned to meditate and discover her inner power. To hibernate and go within.

- **Hawk:** As a messenger, the hawk flew into Kali's life to help her focus and to choose her priorities. With detachment, healing, cleansing, a recollection of her life choices, Kali learned of her gifts of service to humanity. Kali found that it was time for her to become untamed in what she was filled with passion and purpose to create.

- ***Horse:** Freedom was for the taking once horse entered the mind of Kali. Travel, power, stamina, mobility, and speaking her passions became her choices. She would alter her course to adhere to Spirit's calling. No longer desiring to live as a victim, she listened to the voice of her soul with the horse. It was Kali who tamed herself with the horse as her guide.

- **Octopus:** The octopus inspired Kali to travel and follow her dream in her mid-sixties. To embrace what she needed to do and use her intelligence that the creator gave her. She wore many hats as the octopus has many arms. It was now time for her to balance herself and follow her dreams.

- **Elephant:** The fulfillment of Kali's heart was the gift from the elephant. Kali believed she was guided by Spirit to overcome any obstacles in her path with the elephant. It was time for her to become a warrior and step forward to reach her goals in life she had set. Elephant inspired her to speak her truth and love her truth no matter what. Strength as an elephant was part of her belief now.

- ***Wolf:** As a totem animal, wolf is still Kali's main guardian. With the wolf totem, she felt safe and always protected. Wolf has gifted Kali by guiding her forward in her late sixties.

Family, loyalty, friendship, and as a teacher to all of humanity, animal, and plant, Kali awakened with the wolf totem. Once she met her wolf in meditation and discovered it was him all along who guided and protected her, she awakened to her purpose of love for all. To be of service to others, and to offer to heal anyone who journeys alongside her.

Kali smiled to herself as she reflected on the life experiences she enjoyed all these years with these amazing spirit/guide totem animals. She was capable of thinking back to the moment of needing them at difficult times. The sadness of life for her had always been to escape into a book growing up. The challenges of abuse, abandonment, fear, and mental illness could have destroyed Kali at one time. Even death did not scare her, but the pain of the loss of a loved one she suffered secretly at one time.

The path Kali chose to walk with unconditional love was at a very young age. It was this choice that brightened her journey for the difficult moments she had planned prior to her birth. To know and be witness to this game of life delighted her greatly. Kali was more than an avid reader. She simply loved the written word in all its forms. At one time, it was food for her mind and nurtured her soul to ponder the meanings of life in all forms.

Being grateful for all she had in life was a process of belief that she embraced with her heart. Love seemed to her to always be a better choice and very easy. Kali felt that there was a journey in life, and like all journeys, one needs a map to highlight the path to get to their truth. Her past was fueled with little hearts where she chose love. Now in her late sixties, the hearts were growing and pulsating with ascension.

Chapter Five
The Unseen Guidance

Mywolf was sleepy, reflecting on Kali's life through her thoughts but excited for what will come into her world with the faeries She is right now on the cusp of entering this dimension that will guide her to her full power and strength for future years. It is Kali, not Mywolf, that has to do the work. Mywolf has traveled this life experience with her to get her to the faeries and beyond this dimension. What will be, will be, as Mywolf succumbed to rest his head on the moss-filled rock and take a nap.

Mywolf dreamed in Kali's dream as she tried to learn of her purpose years ago. Before bed, she always prayed and asked Spirit what she needed to experience, to send her a sign or at least a message in her dream state to remember in the morning of what her purpose was. Humans, Mywolf thought; her purpose is that which she loves doing. From the moment Kali learned to read and write, her first intention was *I will be a writer of books and a teacher*. She wrote letters, poems, stories as far back as Mywolf remembered. One lifetime she was a teacher. Another time a sage, priest, mystic, and even a monk. Silence and solitude fueled part of many lifetimes. Still, she would ask the same question, "What is my purpose?"

Mywolf remembered that there was a time many years ago where tears fell from Kali's eyes for days because she had not prepared for her life after her children went to live their lives. It was then when she asked for help. It was when Mywolf sent in the owl to guide her further. The owl is a symbol of wisdom and transformation so that one can see in the dark. During this time is when Kali was awakening to her beliefs as a spiritual being.

Mywolf pondered to himself that humans have such a difficult time learning who they are. Even more difficult is the ability to ask for help.

The owl animal totem was a true messenger for Kali and implanted and guided her to her own wisdom and freedom. Mywolf thought all humans had to consider: Was ... that there was a reason for everything in their lives? It is being open to alternative beliefs, spirituality, the unseen world of spirit that helps. No one is ever alone in life! It was the owl as a mentor when it came into Kali's life to help her with her struggles and not seeing what she was meant to do? Who was she meant to be? Did it require schooling? Humans look for certification because of the lack of trust in themselves and others. Kali realized she needed tools and skills to bring her journey to wholeness.

In the past, it had begun with the dog spirit guide because Kali was young and needed to learn how important it was to be faithful, loyal, teaching and noticing guidance. It was years where the dog showed her to be resourceful during difficult times and to choose unconditional love. It was the dog that would rescue her and protect her when needed. When the monkey spirit guide entered her realm for a few years, it was then where Kali discovered light and dark, her ability to change her environment and communication. After that, it was when she learned of her resourcefulness, becoming a gatherer and playful during times of insanity. To support her belief in love as essential for happiness.

Mywolf licked his lips; he felt he did a superb job helping her with the different animal, spirit guides through the years. Many of them she collected—monkeys, there was a time where she had monkeys everywhere. She even wanted to buy a live monkey. But the one that was a favorite of hers was the pig. Everything she owned at one time was a pig or was a picture of a pig or symbol of a pig. For years, she adored the pig as it guided her toward her spiritual strength and learning of being fearless. Today Kali realizes that the pig is a hybrid from lifetimes and lifetimes ago, and because of this, she may be more connected to the pig than anyone else. It guided her years of adoring the pig toward her spiritual strength, and learning of being fearless benefited her. The brief sight of a pig delighted her heart at one time when darkness filled her world.

Mywolf always was on target when it would be time to move on to the next totem animal spirit guide and wean her off the current one. It dawned on Kali one day that she was done with collecting pigs and told everyone she needed no more pigs in her life. Change and growth go hand in hand. It was time to move on to the next totem guide in her journey. And it was the swan with its grace, balance, and innocence, which opened her to a belief in her soul, the grace around her, and began Kali on her journey of transformation and freedom.

When the deer came into her life, she fell in love with the deer's gentle, caring, and kind gracefulness. She was unaware that compassion and peace were the reasons the deer was in her life. The frog jumped right in at a time where she needed cleansing from her past to learn of adaptability and that she would metamorphose into her truth. That there was an elegance in ugliness and that she no longer needed to be inconsistent in life. No longer was it necessary to jump from one thing to another thing.

The owl traveled into her life with a bang over 16 years ago. Everywhere she went, she was witness to the owl, to wisdom, that there was deception in her life and mystery. Secrets filled her mind to find her vision, intuition, and freedom with the owl guiding her. To see was the gift the owl offered her. She saw owls on rooftops, on license plates, in stores, on clothes, and before she realized it, she was purchasing owls for her home.

Mywolf knew of humanity's vulnerabilities and desires and their dreams. He saw in Kali's heart her deepest, deepest wants and desires. For it bears that humans are born with gifts, the truth of self, and a passion and purpose. Mywolf and other totem spirit guides help humans to realize who they are from another dimension. This is the belief in life that we are never, ever alone. We are all guided and supported on this life experience journey as a spiritual being experiencing a human existence.

When the seagull entered, it was a low time in Kali's life when she needed to learn freedom, with her easy-going nature she doubted the creativity that was inside, and the creativity was inside, which she needed to create with passion. She became very resourceful in her life many years ago. It was a time of bonding with Mother Nature again. Traveling to the beach, walking, screaming, singing to the universe of her fears. She was searching for freedom from the life that was silencing her and constricting her dreams. She needed to fly from what was to awaken within her freedom of choice that would set her on her way to the path of her spirituality. Her connection and return to Mother Nature offered her sanity and comfort.

Mywolf guessed at this time, Kali discovered that she had the right to find that which creates freedom of thought. It was a thought he gave to her because she desired freedom from that which no longer served her. Mywolf sent in the turtle to nurture her and to allow her patience, strength, and innocence to allow endurance to follow her into longevity. Kali learned from the turtle that slow but steady progress was the goal. The two cats that came into her life was at a time of struggle that was going on within Kali's life. The cats taught her detachment, magic, and to be independent. To look for the mystery in life was not of the norm. To admit there was a Goddess within she needed to trust.

Mywolf stretched and rose from the ground, excited for Kali and all that was coming in the future. He knew her desires and dreams, and it pleased him to be witness to them all coming true.

Kali is unique, he thought to himself, *for the simple belief she attaches to in the unseen realm.*

Chapter Six
Freedom Arrives

Mywolf thought to himself that timing is everything with humans discovering their purpose and path in life. They look to carry so many unlearned lessons as they travel from lifetime to lifetime with their fears, guilt, shame, grief, lies, illusion, and attachment within their energy fields. When he sent the bear to Kali, it was when what she needed most was courage, willpower, introspection, and great strength to continue traveling her path. The bear was a quick entrance to spark Kali onward. However, Kali felt tender toward the bear and, at one time, wore a necklace of a bear imprint. It was the bear that connected her to Mother Earth, mothering, force, and her inner power while being lovable at the same time.

After the bear, the hawk entered to guide Kali with a message concerning her intuition and guardianship. The hawk was a symbol for her to trust in her visionary power and her healing abilities. It is interesting the time the horse entered. It was a time of complete freedom, mobility, travel, power, and grace that Kali required to exist on her path. An expanded sense of self that Kali needed and relished.

As a woman abused in life from a young age, Mywolf thought, she empowered herself by her will and intent to live a life of passion and purpose. He was witness to it all and now marveled at her strength. He imagined from the guidance of all her spirit/totem animals that he delivered to her when needed in some way, empowered her to believe in herself. This map of life that she walked was unique to her as all are to humans, he imagined.

The octopus confused Kali because octopus symbols surrounded her for months in every place she went, and she had difficulty in understanding why this was happening. It seemed wherever she looked, there was an octopus in pictures, statues, and even on trucks. She bought herself an octopus because she felt there was a reason it was in her life.

It was the octopus that granted Kali the gift of pure intelligence. Mywolf remembered how Kali suffered from low self-esteem and feelings of not being worthy of love because of her abandonment issues. It was a long handling of guiding her to her truth. The tenderness of Kali's mind was embraced by Mywolf daily as he observed her choices. With love as an ability of power for her, she simply connected to the spirit of all the totem/animals he sent.

Her strength, stamina, affection, the sense of history, and pride offered her the time of the elephant around seven years ago. There was deep wisdom that the elephant helped Kali with and continues to do so. With all she needs to remember to carry out her power and wisdom in life, it is a great favor. Most of this life experience, Kali has had a memory that is profound and reliable. With the elephant as her guide, she will continue to share and teach all she learns to aid humanity.

Mywolf stretched his back paws and dug his nails into the ground as he stood up as the spray from the waterfall wet him. What an amazing journey they have been on together. With his loyalty to Kali and perseverance, success, intuition, and his appetite for freedom, he has allowed Kali's appetite to be free. For she and Mywolf are true loners and need their freedom to get inner peace. *What is true freedom*, he thought to himself, *but the ability to become whole?* To live your dreams and to be of service to others on the path one walks.

Mywolf noticed that the sun was setting and a breeze was blowing. He rose to walk to his cave on the other side, high in the woods. Mywolf thought to himself of the greatest gift that Kali owns after lifetimes of trauma and abuse. Licking his salty lips, he felt proud of all she accomplished in this lifetime. It was the gift of unconditional love! She now bestowed it on everyone she met.

Her fears no longer surfaced because they showed her that with her gifts, she would help others.

Years ago, she wanted to share, to make a difference by that which she could do to help another. In her heart, she assumed it was to be a writer, but everything takes time to develop into a plan.

In the human world, Mywolf knew everyone needs a stamp of approval, a degree, or just that they had an understanding of who they were and what they could offer. Mywolf recognized Kali walked her talk, as they say in human society. She was a human being of love and light, and it was this that she shared with all that were sent to her by the universe, from *"the all that is!"*

Mywolf jumped over the waterfall as he headed to his cave. He knew sitting at the waterfall to meditate would help Kali discover a way to travel to other dimensions. Surrounded by Mother Nature and the elementals of the woods would open this door. It was all possible. It was this divine essence of an alternative belief that fueled Kali for years now. She lived and thought outside of the box.

She looked at the entire plan, not just a daily form of one's life. It was always the plan to awaken within Kali all she needed to support in helping to share information that would make a difference in other people's lives. It would be through the power of her fourth chakra, her heart, her ability to express unconditional love.

As Mywolf sauntered toward his cave, he remembered that most of humanity was sound asleep to the lives they were living. Clueless to even examine that an alternative way of living or understanding existed. However, Kali had no fears of traveling outside of the norm. It was part of her gift of unconditional love. She knew of the wounded, beaten, abused, dysfunctional, fearful, shameful, guilty humans in the world. She sensed their fears when they talked or acted in a negative way toward another. In her heart, it was not their truth. It was a way of protecting themselves. She did not anger, judge, or criticize them because she knew they were not aware that they were capable of change in their lives and their stories.

Chapter Seven
The Essence Within

Mywolf had watched as Kali traveled as a child listening to society and the beliefs of her parents until she noticed one day, she was an individual and could make her own choices. There was so much in life she loved doing that others did not. At one time, it was the chores of motherhood that filled her with love, and it was then she knew she was a teacher and that she was being watched by her children. She dug deep within herself to sit, listen, and receive the stories of their day.

She discovered she learned from them and that she respected their needs and dreams. It was over 40 years ago when she did everything she needed to do with love. She was unaware of the spiritual beliefs of life, Mywolf maintained. However, she has connected to the essence within that was her soul's voice even if she was unaware, and chose love as her golden tool.

Mywolf was by his cave. It was dark now. There are no lights in the woods! There was no sound of the waterfall. He heard a coyote call out. Otherwise, there was silence. He walked into his cave to spend the night and to check in on Kali as he did by astral traveling into her dreams. It amazed him every morning when she knew there was something, but she still did not remember her time with him as he guided her on this journey of knowing all she needed to experience as she asked every night before bed. Humans were clearly unaware of their travels during dreamtime to schools and other dimensions.

During the night, Mywolf heard a fierce snowstorm was blowing and that it would cover the woods with a blanket of snow in the morning.

Mywolf opened his eyes to the chill of the morning air and a blanket of snow outside his cave. He licked his paws and cleaned himself as he then stretched. He took a walk outside in the bitter freezing morning air to relieve himself. Once he returned to the cave's warmth, he shook himself free of the snow that had fallen on his coat. He had spent the night with Kali traveling the inner worlds of her mind. *Humans desire to accept the craziest fearful notions*, Mywolf thought to himself.

They searched for freedom and love from all conditions, not realizing that they are born free. They are born as love. It is a social belief that no one is free to live or love as they choose. To love who they are and whoever they choose. To fill with passion stirs their heart and soul. Humans have grouped themselves into categories of what is evil, what is wrong, what they do not accept. Mywolf shared with Kali his beliefs on freedom during the night because he felt it was time for her to teach and share the essence of humanity's right to be free and to love.

Freedom was the greatest of abilities to have. *Freedom* allows one to perceive their truth, to believe in themselves, and notice nothing is ever wrong with the laws of the universe if one lives free. No one has the ability or the power to tell another human how to live, dress, work, what school to go to, or even whom to love. Religion, race, and status in life have nothing to do with one's freedom. These are just part of the games of life that teach how to exist as humanity to learn acceptance of one another.

Mywolf knew everyone comes to life to learn lessons they designed to expand the growth of their soul. There is no wrong in anyone to try to learn the lesson of love by opening one's heart. To realize one is free is to believe in the self, the passion within, and the joy and happiness when peace is part of one's daily existence. *Freedom* is to experience you are not here to make another happy by making yourself small and powerless. Freedom is being true to oneself and how one thinks, speaks, and acts by harming no one. It takes work and sometimes lifetimes to learn that change is part of life, and with change, growth will then open a belief; it is the right of humanity, all humanity to be free. Unity and oneness are the paths to the discovery of self.

Most of the night, Mywolf traveled with Kali to help her learn freedom. He knew she understood the basics, but it was a human belief of control she battled against most of her life. Humans accepted this right to control one another through their fears, guilt, shame, and lies. If one chooses any of these in their life, they can never be free. To develop and understand that anger, fear, and resentment toward another because another is not doing as they are demanding of them. *Humans*, Mywolf thought to himself, *are their own worst enemy.* Any of the above does not define love. Love is joy, inner peace, happiness, magical, and blissful. Humans do not comprehend the words: "To live and let live!" Mywolf watched from his dimension and saw much abuse and attack on each other, and then they say, "I love you!"

Kali had developed freedom of her own to allow sanity to be part of her day. It became a tool of wisdom she discovered within, because of Mywolf, that allowed her to find she had rights. It was years ago when she studied the blueprints of the soul, the chakras, and experienced for the first time in her mid-life she, as a human, had rights. These energy centers within the body are invisible to the eye and carry with them the emotions that trigger disease in the body because the organs are along the body where the chakras sit. These wheels spin in full clockwise motion when balanced, centered, and grounded.

The body has many chakras, but seven concern humanity.

- Appearing at the base of the spine is the first chakra and the right to have and be.
- Two, at the sacral, is the right to enjoy.
- Three, at the solar plexus, is the right to act.
- Four, at the heart, is the right to love.
- Five, at the throat, is the right to speak.
- Six, between the brows, is the right to see.
- Seven, at the crown of the head, is the right to learn.

Mywolf remembered how foreign the chakras were to Kali at one time. Then when she studied them and learned how they affected the human body, she treasured their power. To learn that she had "seven rights" she was born with that went with the seven chakras and her organs and body, impelled her forwards on her journey. It was these chakras that filled her with the first twinkling thoughts of her freedom.

It was mid-day now as Mywolf journeyed out of his cave. The sun was shining, and the snow was melting. He needed to stretch and move his body after being in the cave for all these hours, just as humans needed to do. Mywolf walked out of the cave and looked for food to eat. As he realized all this teaching and insight with Kali, he had forgotten to eat.

Chapter Eight
World of Spirit

The greatest pleasure for Mywolf, as a spirit guide, was his ability to travel with Kali and to receive her thoughts. Many humans were not aware that the spirit hears, sees, and knows everything happening in one's life position. When one connects to the spirit world and trusts in life and what meets the eye, a magical, mystical door opens beyond this dimension of life on earth. It was Kali's choice to seek the unknown through positive affirmations, prayer, journaling, meditation, aromatherapy, metaphysical belief, and to read many spiritual books that had propelled her forward toward knowing and experiencing Mywolf. Mywolf would lie by the waterfall in the woods relaxing and just think of Kali to recall her thoughts.

Mywolf sat on top of the waterfall to check in with Kali and to peek into her inner thoughts. Her rituals were many, and her thoughts always tried to comprehend why people did what they did and why. Human behavior intrigued her. Mywolf knew of the power of knowing we are all one. There is no separation. No detachment is possible. What affects Kali affects everyone else in the world just as another's actions affect her. Humans were clueless as to this "superpower" they owned with their thoughts, words, and actions. The simplicity of this was that if I hurt you with my words, I am hurting myself. Mywolf connected his energy to hers now and recovered yesterday's thoughts…

"Strange this life looks. The fears and hate filled many. I recognize it is only a pattern they create. Parents want children, and then they abuse them and demand to control their lives even as adults. A parent was the deal handed

to children to learn from as an example, with the ability to change what did not work for you yesterday, today. Few opened their eyes to look. To understand this was not to be. I witness the large picture in life. I wonder why?"

Mywolf allowed Kali her privacy at times as she drifted off to sleep especially. When she would sleep and awaken to the experience of lifetimes filled with love, joy, and happiness, Kali was delighted. Her thoughts were always questioning life. Mywolf listened in to the rambles of her thoughts... *Much is an unknown sequence daily in life. Everyone has forgotten who they are.*

Kali was aware of the mystical and magical world of her past, which filled her daily. At times, it was possible for her to escape this dimension in the day's middle and jump to the 5th dimension.

No one could touch her when she traveled forward. There was a freedom she did not explain but understood in her heart it was to be. She suspected it was necessary to survive in this cynical world that surrounded her. It was an illusion and not a real world for her. Kali had many friends she summoned up to communicate with and guide her. Besides Mywolf, there was her elemental body she named Joy and the Angels and Ascended Masters.

Kali slipped into the real world and returned to a world of magical, mystical surroundings. She developed this pattern of her own to comprehend life. For humanity accepted only what they sensed with their five senses. Many did not grasp their own intuition or insight. To experience as their truth of being. Kali understood that now in the world called earth, peace can develop only with a change of belief. Forgiveness of self and everyone else was essential.

Mywolf had whispered into her mind during the night to pay attention. To the movies. The books and songs! Truth is all around humanity. The science fiction stories, the aliens amongst us! These writers show what the fact is. Kali slept well during the night and then awakened as if dropped back into her bed. She waited to recall her dream. In her heart, she went to school and returned to a mystical time. A dimension is so close but yet so far to the human eye. Kali knew life was love and that only with choosing love one eased their ego. The roar of the ego can be a witness to daily life by the fear, anger, and hate projected amongst humanity.

A belief stirred her mind daily of living. She understood this other way of life. She trusted in faeries, dragons, elves, elementals, and crystal skulls. It was a real-world experienced by Kali.

Those who called her a dreamer or extreme in her thoughts did not recognize what she did. She could walk up to a tree, place her palms on its bark, and appreciate its heartbeat. When she awakened in the morning and stepped outside to say," Hello" to Mother Nature, she felt acknowledged. There was an essence around her that enabled Kali to communicate and experience all these mystical extremes. For Kali, it was the real world.

Mywolf stood right next to Kali, and she felt his body. If she closed her eyes, she would recognize him. This filled her with a deep love of gratitude for this friend she had. Sometimes she looked at a man or woman and knew their pain, knew their fear, and experienced wounds that inflicted them daily. It was at these times that Kali was thankful for her connection to the spirit world.

The spirit beings, nature beings, and elementals encouraged her. It was their guidance and her belief in them that allowed her to accept humans filled with fear. She had become witness that it was their ego they clung to as their truth. It was this belief that kept them stuck in fear and pain daily.

The journey of challenges was no more. Life had allowed her to open her eyes to this world that needed help. Fear, Shame, Guilt, Grief, Lies, Illusion, and Attachment were the demons humanity created. Kali's truth was to share information and help humans strive for their awakening. Upon awakening, one would be led to their ascension. It was essential to the planet. Humans and the spirit world needed to join forces. Kali felt this pull in her heart that change was necessary for humanity.

Christians prayed to God, Angels, and Saints. They trusted in their prayers being answered. It was their reason for going to church, for not eating meat on Fridays during Lent. It was their sacraments that held them together as a congregation in prayer and worship. Other religions had their rituals and beliefs to join them as a congregation.

Yet, man has allowed these communities to hate one another and be angry at their choices. Mankind has the ability to be brainwashed by a societal belief in looking for answers outside themselves. Kali learned early on that all the answers she ever needed were within her. It was this deep connection to herself that has allowed her to thrive in the spirit world.

There was a teaching within Kali that stirred her soul into action. It looked to Kali that she straddled two worlds but craved the magical, mystical, mystery one the most. She was an introvert and loved her silence and connection to spirit daily. It pleased her and filled her with inner peace to acknowledge that she knew she was not alone. She wondered why she could understand this while others did not, could not, or would not. She tried sharing her beliefs but knew when to stop talking and realize when she was not capable of helping another.

Her greatest gift she received was that she could only help someone who wants help. All is energy in life and Kali believed humanity could raise their vibration with love and kindness.

Kali now knew of her spirit guide totem animal, who she named Mywolf through a meditation. She knows she receives information and thoughts from him, and in doing so, she has traveled through her life. This life experience has unleashed all the changes, growth, and expansion she received from Mywolf. Her thoughts are her guides, and it looks to her being supervised by another at all times. She has learned to listen to the tiniest of thoughts she receives and to act.

This is what others called intuition, insight, or guidance. Kali calls it, Mywolf!

Chapter Nine
The Temple of Love

The "Temple of Love" filled with a magnificent glow as Kali entered her dream state. There was so much joy in her heart, she felt in awe. Kali travels to the "Temple of Love" at night. She embraces all in this other dimension. The essence of life begins in the "Temple of Love." Kali knows of the human belief that is black and white. What they see? All they perceive. How many live their life? Part of the altering is to decide that nothing is as it implies.

Kali realized as a young child, that life was fascinating. Her heart opened to the challenges she recognized, which were the lessons she needed to learn. It looked magical to her. To love was the basis. When one has a wish for reading spiritual books and writing that fueled them daily, this was a beginning? It implied a game of sorts to walk the map of one's life for her. Seeking to figure that moment in time when the destination will be reached finally. For Kali, it arrived late in life.

However, Kali perceived within her being, there was a quality a divine intelligence she connected with. At the time, she understood it was a light within that needed sustenance. Her dreams and her waking state filled her with thoughts that only she could determine as a truth. It was at that moment where she determined her truth was to travel a spiritual alternative belief system of sharing information.

It was a road filled with difficulties she traveled as her path. Others in her life had many fears and demons they were struggling with. Kali had no demons and no fears at this time.

She acknowledges Mywolf as the totem animal that traveled along her side for lifetimes. It was his connection to her that strengthened her on this journey.

The simple belief to discover that one is never ever alone. To ask and receive is her greatest accomplishment.

The wisdom she discovered from within is her gift to share. She no longer has any doubt. Life is lessons, light, love, and happiness. Many choose not to pay attention. To hate, be unhappy, and in fear is their choice. She does not take this personally. Her days are active and full after her nighttime travels. Sometimes she knows she slips into a dimensional insight during the day and misses a present moment. It is at these times she smiles to herself and laughs. Kali straddles both spirituality and humanity daily. Life is this journey of discovery of self that incorporates complete freedom from the ego.

She heard a whisper from Mywolf that there were many Temples to discover. It was an acknowledgment on her part she was ready for the wisdom they held within. Kali received the thought; all the Temples were of the mind. The essence of existence was based on sacredness. Kali believed her home was a "Temple of Sacredness," because being of service to others was Sacred.

There were lifetimes of eternal wisdom to grasp, which were filled with gratitude. The "Temple of Love" is the first to discover. In doing so, the wisdom of lifetimes ignites, and no turning back is possible. Once this door swings open, life as a human straddles life as a Spirit. To find and believe in one's heart, true love is when one embraces love no matter what the plight is. Humans are here to learn of their eternal mind's wisdom through the doors of the Temples.

Kali and Mywolf were both amazed that humans were unaware of the elegance of life that surrounds them daily. Every day is a gift called the present to notice life. To awaken to a blissful way of being. To choose a new way of believing in thought, word, and action. Life is a chance to appreciate by acknowledging the value of Mother Nature daily.

Humans see the sun and enjoy the warmth in the air and express that today is a great day. Most are clueless to even a sunny day. All days are a great day when one is present to themselves. It is the Sacred of life that unfolds in a day that one must adhere to with love. Sacredness is for all to experience every day when one acknowledges that life filled with the ego is not real, but an illusion.

Humans have a mentality of competition from a young age. It is such a way of living one's life that enables a thought to get settled within that one needs to be the best. There is no love or joy if the struggle to compete in everything is all that one desires. No Temple doors can open by such a belief structure. If fear is present, there can be no love. The two are separate ways of living one's life. They can never be present at the same time. You either love or fear!

Mywolf watched the workings of Kali's mind as she slept. All humans traveled to school while they slept, but most were not aware of doing so. Dream time was the mind's journey of awakening one to their truth slowly.

Love of self is the beginning of loving another, Kali realized. The open heart of self allows healing and light to flow. The "Temple of Love" radiated with the emerald green essence of this healing. One needs to choose love first to change.

Chapter Ten
The Temple of Joy

During the night, Kali traveled to experience the "Temple of Joy." Once Kali discovered the Temples, she understood the process after experiencing the "Temple of Love" by the way Love offered one to fill with an inner Joy. So, the "Temple of Joy" opens wide its doors for entrance. Kali thought to herself that there were numerous times during the day she felt her heart fill with the sense of Joy. She could drive and notice the delicacy of the trees and find Joy. She may look out her window and listen to the birds singing in the trees, look up and fill with Joy. This "Temple of Joy" delighted her senses. There looked to be an amazing volume of Joy to experience daily.

- Joy is an emotion in the heart of Kali's unconditional love.
- Joy is the essence within Kali that lifted the mind.
- Joy is the simplicity of life that Kali delighted in daily.

A smile formed on her lips as she considered her connection to Spirit. So slight but still present for her to say, *"Thank you."* Kali filled her hours with this simple prayer daily. It was her way of knowing how special, grand, and enjoyable her life experience is. Two words, *"Thank you,"* were in her mind as respect for *"the all that is."* She realized that in choosing love and forgiving others, change was the gift. Every day, she discovered another facet of herself. It was the realms she traveled to that guided her discoveries. There were no mistakes. Life today was because there can be no mistakes. All is, as it is, at this time on earth.

After a morning of discovering the woods and meditating by her waterfall, Kali was beaming with an essence of another world. There was a calmness within her soul as she hiked into the woods further for the first time. As Kali hugged the biggest tree she ever saw, she felt connected to the Spirit of the tree. Then she wondered to herself that this was how life had been at one time. Land, trees, animals, and the sun shining fiercely in the sky. No noise, no internet, no television, no cars, which meant silence was the journey.

As she realized she had lived at one time within this silence and refinement, she felt sad. The world today was a busy, noisy place filled with more to do than the average person could manage. The peace that many needed was in these woods or in any place where there was Mother Nature to heal the rush of life they now experienced. Kali felt joy in her heart as she had this land, forest, and waterfall to nourish herself. There was this energy she could not put her finger on, but she supposed it to be that of Spirit, Life, and Love.

Mywolf looked into the mind of Kali and felt her sorrow and sadness for humanity. He knew she was getting ready for another teacher in life that could soon empower her to bring forward *"a new humanity."* Mywolf felt happy that progress was being created during this lifetime for Kali.

As life is not as many believe it to be ever, Mywolf felt honored to have been part of this life journey with Kali. His chest swelled up as he trotted back to the cave for the night as Kali left the woods. He could sense her Joy. He was proud of her!

Kali was unaware of the truth of her spirituality from traveling to the "Temple of Joy" and the essence of its pink ray of healing. Joy was followed by the essence of happiness that stirs deep within the self to be acknowledged.

Humans were clueless as to how to be happy and what would make them happy. Kali had been gifted sight into these Temples to share the truth of existence in life by going within for the answers.

Chapter Eleven
The Temple of Happiness

The "Temple of Happiness" was a thought that filled Kali's mind when she awoke. Happiness? Yes, she imagined that Love, Joy, and Happiness was what she felt. Mywolf knew that Kali was on a path of discovery that few ventures to go into ever. Kali loved to study. The books she consumed daily and the words that filled her mind encouraged her to seek more. One book leads to five books. A mention in one book of another inspired Kali to read said books!

- She devoured books as a person dying of thirst.
- She needed to see and admire the written word.
- Something filled her within the essence of these books.
- She desired to study human behavior exploring the teachers of many books.
- The fear, anger, and hate humans expressed intrigued her.
- Many lose control of themselves by a minor word or action, and she wanted to understand why.
- She believed the answers she needed were to be found in words thought, spoken, and read.

No one could make another happy, Mywolf told her. Happiness equals choices chosen daily. Happiness resulted from choosing the love of God. Fear is the ego, and there can be no Happiness. In a world that struggles with truth, no one comprehends *"free will."*

Choose another way to be. Sounds simple but difficult when the ego roars its hate.

Many are unhappy, hateful, and filled with fear! Kali wondered why they did not choose another way. In learning through the books she devoured and the nightly visits to the real magical/mystical world, Kali discovered that the ego separated most from their Divine Self. It was a talent of the ego to fill the mind with the belief that one was a victim, that trust was not a choice, and abuse was the answer.

It was the mind of the ego that defers one from their truth and to choose a life of this belief in protecting themselves from others, no matter what the condition or reason may be. The ego does not believe in Love, Kindness, or Happiness. The ego fears the Love of God and unity.

In fact, the discovery of patterns that may have developed to protect themselves is amazing. Who are they protecting themselves from, Kali wondered? If everyone is Love, there can be no fear. Fear stems from the ego. The ego stems from one's personality.

Parents fill with fear and raise children that develop a pattern of protection from their parents to exist. The ego is roaring. The ego rises to the condition of fear, and the truth of the child is no longer. This child will grow up feeding their ego until no resemblance to Love exists. These are the humans that abuse others with their words and actions. They are fearful, angry, and hold on to their pain as they struggle with a world they created. Where no Love is, there can be no God. This is not the real world.

The reality of life is that if one is not filled with Happiness daily, they are struggling with the mind of the ego. The ego has to be balanced and trained to look at life with an open heart. When the heart closes, it is due to fear, not Love. The ego/personality is generationally gifted to many by their parents. To be a Happy parent than one will find a Happy child.

However, at times there are two parents, and one can be filled with Happiness while the other is filled with fear. The child is raised in an atmosphere of choosing one over the other. Kali believed this was the path of many children today. It was a search for Happiness that was individual for all. That was *"free will."*

Kali discovered early that forgiveness of these humans was necessary for her spirituality to expand. Change is essential for growth. The choice is *"free will."* If something is not working, change equals one to choose again. Many get stuck in the embrace of their ego and refuse to try another way.

Mywolf and Kali traveled a journey together of sacredness and truth. Mywolf, as a spirit animal, knows of the pleasures and Joy of not living in an illusion. The mind that is real is abundant with the truth. It is not the mind many cling to, but more to their ego. The "Truth of Self" is choosing to forgive those in pain, move on, and realize "Love is God." "God is Love." "Love is all there is!"

Chapter Twelve
The Temple of Peace

When Kali took pen to paper in a journal and did her morning rituals of meditation and prayer, she developed inner Peace. The "Temple of Peace" is part of the divine plan after someone experiences the other Temples. Kali perceived that Love, Joy, and Happiness led to Peace. She marveled at the ability she owned today. She trusted in the Divine and chose Love.

The gift was to acknowledge that her mind was in her control. She could learn and figure out for herself. She did not have to follow others. *"Free will"* gave her the ability to appreciate Mywolf and Spirit. There was a tremendous inner Peace for Kali when she trusted in God. For this lifetime, she chose to always go within no matter what the plight. Mywolf whispered to her to take a break, meditate, go for a walk, free your mind. Choose again. Kali always listened to Mywolf's guidance.

Mywolf watched from a distance while Kali sat by the waterfall and meditated. Inner Peace poured from her essence. It made Mywolf's heart skip a beat. She has arrived. She has connected to Spirit. He can see the faeries around Kali and knows in his own heart she senses them too. In time, she, too, will witness their vision and partnership.

Mywolf watched further as she took out her journal after her meditation. He could be in her mind and witness her thoughts. The value of being a Spirit guide had many benefits. Kali had a way of making sense of the human world through her journal and her Spirit guides, which always inspired her. As she looked around as if sensing Mywolf, she took her pen to paper and wrote.

"The responsibilities of my life were overwhelming. Knowing we are born with inner wisdom, I began a search for knowledge. I wanted more because I knew there had to be more. I traveled a path of discovery into the dimensions of myself to find who I am. Fragile to yesterday's fears, I forced myself to become a seeker. I craved another me.

The voice within that I connected to lead my journey forward. To share love was my quest, no matter that I felt unloved. Seen as a crazy woman, I held my head up high. The journey unfolded, but I grasped life and what I intended. The truth of life for everyone is to embrace Love. Love is everything there ever is in life to claim.

I learned how gifted we are when we arrive. My gift took me a lifetime to discover. A destiny to teach Love as my choice. To help another to choose to Love. Where Love is, there can never be fear. I released the fears that screamed at me. Guilt, shame, anger, hate, and criticism are not of Love.

- *Love is to meditate, pray, write, and read spiritual books.*
- *Love waits for me in the grace of Mother Nature.*
- *Love is the wind that blows the trees while the birds sing.*
- *Love is the act of a walk, swim, or even hugging a tree.*
- *Love is the babies that come from my children.*

The human wants more. The Spirit wants nothing. Today, I am loving my life because of the journey I have lived. To release yesterday brought me to my truth, purpose, and passion. There has to be more to life. Life is not what we imagine it to be, but what we cannot even imagine it to be.

I stepped out of the nothingness of the life that held me bound. The path was full of thorns and rocks. Until the voice within whispered at me to try. There could be sadness for what could never be unless I searched for that something more. It was worth the try for me. Is this the plan, the destiny, but to try?

Truth is the greatest of gifts we own. Then we find a means to protect ourselves and incorporate fear as a choice. Choose Love ran through my mind. I grasped it and held on tight. A switch within lit up my being and beamed Love outwards. I smiled and thanked the unseen."

It delighted Mywolf, the gift of Kali's writing. Life has awakened in her the discovery of truth. Most humans, like Kali, were unaware for years that they were not living their truth. Connection to spirit embraces one's truth to develop. In doing so, change, growth, expansion, and freedom become essential. It was the inner Peace that poured from Kali that Mywolf embraced. To let the fears and pain of another have no effect on her was the greatest of her lessons learned.

Chapter Thirteen
The Temple of Manifestation

It was a few weeks before Kali returned to the waterfall. Mywolf was always with her and watched her every move daily. He noticed it was difficult for Kali to stay in the world of humanity. Joy filled her heart and soul when she traveled into the realm of spirit. The writing was a great blessing for her to release the past and to choose another way of belief.

It was early morning now because Kali had noticed that sleep was scarce. Her mind was full of stories she suspected she needed to tell. There was this inner urge to help humanity raise their vibration. It called to her and beckoned her to make a plan, act, and offer nourishment and Love to the many filled with fear. Words were part of her toolbox, and Kali connected through the written word with many.

Taking her pen to paper, she began.

"In reflection, I discovered yesterday's purpose and that at one time, I had a dream. Without realizing it, my dreams were coming true. She smiled as she remembered that nothing lasts forever—change will come! I held this note out to another. Recognizing in my heart how life had molded me as a child, women, and mother. My freedom was to step out of the mold. Yesterday, the tears fell. Today, joy fills my world. Happiness is my bliss. Tears of laughter wet my face.

I heard an inner call from the depths of my being. As a sparkling light in the darkness of my life. It was then I moved toward my future. I walked out the door of everything that was no longer me. I began a journey of discovery into my dreams.

For any change in life, everyone needs to choose an action. Ridiculously, to write, but today I see the truth. Dreams come true.

First, one has to begin a dream to set it free. Call it passion or purpose, but everyone has ideas. Stuff we are good at doing. Cherishing our positive thoughts leads us toward dreams of what may be. It matters not the path we take. What matters is that we release what no longer serves us with love. Embracing what one is doing is the real key to a positive, fulfilled, Happy life.

Surrender is the way. Just surrender to anything that is not love.

Gifts sometimes come. It blessed me to receive many. Truth, freedom, and my voice empowered me to be the woman I am today. Walking out of who I had been helped me end the pain and sorrow of a lifetime not prepared for by me. I enjoyed myself yesterday, but then it was no longer to be. Children grow up and leave the nest. I needed to set them free.

I looked within with tears of sorrow for that which had ended, I asked for guidance. Change and growth became my path to study what was to be. I listened to that inner voice that led me on this new journey of acting. A widening path to a divine plan. I opened my heart and arms to the knowledge I craved. Knowing within was the wisdom waiting for me.

To write, teach, and to be of service had been the dream for as long as I could remember. I discovered within a new me to share with the world. Who knew this was for me? I loved the chores of motherhood that are no longer mine to bask in. Today, I am offering Light and Love to help another.

I reflect on the years of this life I learned to embrace. There is always a free choice. With freedom comes forgiveness and release of the past to stay true to the present. There can be no future where there is anger, sorrow, or fear for what cannot be any longer. It is the growth of the body, mind, and soul that is an absolute dream to aim for in life..."

My wolf walked across the waterfall and listened in on Kali's thoughts. As a Spirit guide and totem animal, a wolf to be exact, he relished his connection with Kali and how his guidance in her Divine plan to awakening had led her to this moment of Manifestation. He knew all it took for her to believe in herself. All she had to forgive! The tears and abuse she had endured to realize she was a Divine Child of God and had the power of Manifestation all along.

Time was approaching, where Kali needed to move on without him. He could not guide or help her anymore. Another's voice waited to connect with

Kali. The Manifestation of her dreams, thoughts, magic, synchronicity, and teachers have brought Kali to this place. "A Key to the Unseen World" awaited as the teaching for her to share with the society of humanity to ascend. This Manifestation is a truth of who Kali is in her life. It is a connection that has granted her insight into how humans, in general, need to simply ask to receive help. In doing so, one is never ever alone once they believe in this power they possess.

Chapter Fourteen
The Temple of Healing

Kali thought to herself of the years she wrote poetry during the difficult challenges she faced yesterday. Whenever there was fear, chaos, criticism, anger of any kind, Kali took pen to paper and wrote a poem. In this way, she learned a deep form of therapy of Healing herself at a young age. Poetry was a blessing in disguise for her and poured from her soul. It looked easy for her to whip out a poem that made sense to the moment and how she was thinking. For Kali, it was this form of Healing herself for years that encouraged her to release the past through this form of writing and becoming free in doing so.

Mywolf waited patiently to hear Kali's thoughts; as she awakened this day, out came her journal, and a poem came to life just like that on the paper. Mywolf sat down to observe her thoughts, and Kali began with a sense that this was a release for her that will help in her Healing process.

"All is well—I am safe!
I heard you whisper to me
Open your eyes and see
The beauty of everyday
Are in the thoughts and words you say!

The voice within an echo of me
Struggling to be free
Encouraging me forward to my dreams
Repeatedly to stop the screams!

All is well—I am safe!
Has been my mantra for years
All is well—I am safe!
Has released my fears!

A whisper from deep within saved me
To reveal my greatness and set me free
The soul knows what the body fears
As I no longer shed yesterday's tears!
I can Change! I can Grow! I can Create!

The whisper of my Soul filled my mind
After years of thinking I was blind
I did Change! I did Grow! I did Create!
Now I sit in wonder of you free
Filled with Love for Life, even for you and me

My mantra all these years embraced the unknown
And in doing so, releasing me from having a breakdown!
Positive thought and action led the way
The Discovery of Self that allowed me to have a say
I had trembled for years to find my voice
Filled with not knowing if I even had a choice!

All is well—I am safe
Has been my mantra for years
All is well—I am safe
Has released my fears!

The pain, sorrow, and regret inside
Was plain to see, and I could not hide
From the torments of yesterday's exhaustion
I was lifted up by the essence of intention!
Clueless at one time who I was to be
I walked forward into a world that nourished me

Spirituality grabbed me in its arms of Light
It was then my eyes opened wide to true Sight.
One must travel forward and forget the past
It's all about one's lessons learned that should last

As the essence of Spirit fills the Soul to expand
Into the universe of life and to all woman and man!
Discovery of Self is the importance of Sight
It joins one with the essence of belief in flight
Once the connection is made, Joy nurtures the Soul. There is no turning back
as one becomes Whole!

All is well—I am safe!
Has been my mantra for years
All is well—I am safe!
Has released my fears!"

Mywolf puffed out his chest as he heard the words in Kali's head as she wrote. Without realizing it, she had heard his whispers and wrote a poem for him. His Love and support were his greatest gift to her. When he volunteered to be her totem animal Spirit guide, he knew many lifetimes of offering her Love were part of the plan. The challenges she had chosen, the parents she picked, and the family and friends in her circle extremely challenged life.

Mywolf and Kali knew of the cleansing of one's karma by the actions and choices during lifetimes lived. The transformation is a belief that what you do in this lifetime, I will do to you in the next lifetime to cleanse myself of negative karma. If I murder you today, then in the next lifetime, you will murder me. They base life on *"free will,"* and the choices humanity lives by, Mywolf figured. However, humanity was clueless that every thought, word, and action was a choice. Kali's Healing has now begun!

Chapter Fifteen
The Temple of Opening

Kali was always reflecting on her journey and life. When she was by her waterfall, she felt deeply connected to the elements. There was a deep energy and spirit field presence that grabbed her mind and soul to look within for answers. Her mind sounded to her to be filled with questions, dialog, and answers to a Divine plan she was part of daily. Taking pen to paper rescued her from her mind as a release. If she put the words on paper, then she could understand with Love in her heart the amazing life experience she was taking part of in life. Kali always expected when a door was to open, she needed to walk through it and check out why it opened. Now she realized that these doors were her Temples she needed to experience within.

There were moments when Kali thought she dreamed the dream of words during the night that then surfaced in her journal in the morning. Within her Spirit, she could sense the essence of her Soul and the nourishment it guided her toward through the written word. It filled her journal with the thoughts of her Soul and that which filled her and nurtured her daily. Her favorite place to write in was going into the woods, knowing Mother Nature's embrace waited, and the true world of Spirit surrounded her.

Today she had just meditated, and Mywolf sat by her feet. She could not see him but could accept the essence of his Spirit warming her legs. It was a cool morning, and the waterfall was in full blast. Picking up the sound of the birds chirping in the trees, she knew not far away a deer waited. Her favorite time of the year to go to the waterfall was when it snowed.

The whiteness and coldness empowered her to pay attention and appreciate Mother Nature's true beauty, which was all around.

She began…

"There was an inner void I questioned. Terrified to find out my beliefs and who I was. Is my life up to this moment generational? Was I programmed by the women who came before me? I looked within to Discover my truth. To embrace that which was my Power, Passion, and Purpose. I sat in silence. I learned to connect to the Light within, to listen, and my place in the world unfolded. There was an inner being of self that led me to my truth.

Although my voice was low, it had waited for me. I raised my hand in jubilation and into eternity. Knowing within held the answers. I discovered the reasons and purpose for life. I asked. I received. I heard. Time to release yesterday's fear. It was at this moment I found my strength. Or, was it the courage to live my existence?

I was cracked wide open yesterday. Filled with fears from another's way of maintaining. Never mine to choose. As if gifted to absorb. I stopped the pain, and I opened the closed door.

Remaining present to my existence empowered me. I could not change the past path I traveled. Or, another to see. Love is the key to choose daily. Any other choice closes the door to fear.

Today, I smile at the memory of what was. Happy and filled with Joy for the self. I learned freedom is for everyone to embrace. Life is full of Passion and Purpose in our existence here.

Peering at life with eyes from within to appreciate ourselves allows Miracles. To live my truth today, I needed to open the door. Remaining in silence, staying present allows Change and Growth to manifest. I can never turn back now. My life can never be as it was once since I connected to the Light within my essence.

We each have our Light to connect to one day. Our unique door to open and walk through to tomorrow. Forgiveness holds our hand to walk toward the door and in choosing Love. At that moment, happiness comes. As humans, we are fragile. Many are overwhelmed by the responsibilities and demands of life. Struggling to guess why others are as they are. In Silence, the guessing stops. We can learn to Forgive and Trust. Everyone has a story; many carry fears, while others manifest chaos in their lives. I learned the message to receive can only be when we seek to find why. It is time to open the closed door!"

Kali read over her journal words and smiled. The simplicity of her life appeared when she knew there had to be more to living this life. Kali was never driven to be an active person or to need more material objects in her life. Content to read a book or to enjoy her chores around her house while raising her family, she had a motto to do everything with Love. For years, she went with the flow of life daily. What will be, will be! She grew to resemble her father in attitude in that regard, and this pleased her.

It was enjoyable to live in this manner, but yet her husband was the complete opposite of her. He needed a plan. To learn where he was going and when. Then he needed to recognize where he was going after he returned. Kali discovered years ago that she was very adaptable. What mattered to her husband did not matter to her, so she went with the flow. He knew she was happiest with a book. As different as they were, they complemented one another only because Kali felt part of the Spirit world today and had an enormous Open Heart filled with Love.

Mywolf stretched out his legs and stood up stiffly. He knew for today, Kali was done writing as she walked back up the hill to the house. The wind was picking up again. Mywolf wanted to get to his cave for the night to rest. Mywolf felt honored to be a wise animal Spirit guide for Kali through these years. He felt in his heart, they had raised her vibration and that his time with her was coming to a close. Sad that he had to return to his realm and let her find her way in her dimension. Yet, he realizes what she needed to help humanity with was essential to life.

He reflected on the lifetimes they had shared with her other animals and their wisdom that were unseen and guided her journey. The most interesting of her spirit guides was the recent one that has been popping up in her view. Mywolf did not send the porcupine, so he himself is interested because this totem animal Spirit guide keeps showing itself to Kali.

He knew the message was for her to free herself from guilt and shame. To fill herself with the sight of a child and to turn to her inner mother and father when she felt in need of protection. For Kali to appear safe! There is no need to assume shame for showing her true self to the world. Mywolf knew the woods calmed her and let Kali reflect on her journey. Her challenges were not hers but of others that could take her Joy away in a quick second.

Mywolf felt the challenges of being human. The fears that Kali faced because many did not and chose not to be open-minded as she was. Her

Laughter and Joy, when in the woods, was a Light from within her Soul. She could Dance, Laugh, Sing, and enjoy being free again in the woods. When Kali returned home, hours away from the woods, it was a transition that rattled her, and she ached from her heart to return to the woods. To Kali, it stood to be a magical/mystical/mystery forest of Light, Love, and Serenity, Mywolf considered.

Mywolf was proud of her accepting the Temples as the moments in her life where she personally chose another way to be and live. The "Temple of Opening" was the most difficult because within this Temple was the total release of doubt of self. Kali was powerful in going with the flow of life, but underneath she held close to her the doubt of others. Once she realized it was another's belief in doubt in life to cling to, and not hers, the "Temple of Opening" flew open its doors.

It was time for him to pack up his bags and leave from this part of the journey they have traveled. He imagined he shall now watch from the side and let another take over the Golden Reins of inspiring and guiding Kali to her passion and purpose in this life completely. To fulfill her mission! He had prepared her for these unique gifts she possessed to develop and share with humanity. To Teach! To Inspire! To Guide! To Ascend!

Chapter Sixteen
The Temple of Magic

Kali opened her eyes and tried to remember where she was sleeping. Where was she? In the woods or at home? She struggled with the bright light shining through and knew she was home. As she lay in bed, closing her eyes to place herself in the woods, she relaxed. Traveling farther into the woods than ever before, she felt a deeper connection. The semblance of Purity and life without humans engulfed her. The sounds of the trees, birds, and even the dripping of the waterfall excited her. At this moment, all she could do was laugh and smile at the memory and fill herself with Joy.

Her life felt different as if she needed to connect to the woods and the animals for a reason. Kali could not wrap her mind around it, but there was an essence or presence that beckoned to her to be aware. Pay attention to these woods. Pay attention to life. Sadness took up a corner of her heart, and she needed to meditate. In doing so, she calmed herself, settled into her own body, and reconnected with her Spirit guides. Mywolf was missing, and she wondered why.

Kali traveled a journey of deep imagination where she was from another time and place her entire existence. Thrilled with magical, alien, and supernatural imaginings. Reflecting on her dad, she fantasized that he had always resembled an owl to her. In looking at an image of an owl, she saw her dad. Someone has written that dog and cat owners resemble their pets. Kali smiled because she knew her dad was a wise man and guide for her on this life's journey.

The heartbeat she felt in her chest had changed since she traveled into the woods. Life was different and filled with Magic. Kali felt a deep connection to the Unseen worlds, dimensions, and realms. Unable to be a witness with Sight, Kali had a deep appreciation, a knowing there was another world in her world. Maybe a part of her world that filled her with Peace. Many times, during the day, she witnessed a fast shadow or breeze from the corner of her eye. She was never ever alone. Kali knew there was more to life. Compared to the human life she belonged to daily.

Her day was starting. In a few weeks, she shall return to the woods. She knew the waterfall and her woods waited for her. Her Rituals sustained her until that time. It had to be this way. She lived here and traveled there as a retreat from normal life by going into the woods. She had her dreams, the moon, stars, and sun to connect to daily.

Kali felt off today as if there was a change on the planet. There was a chill she could not describe. Something was going to happen. She always felt before a change that change was coming. Whether it be Happy or Sad, it required a Change in Growth to manifest.

Mywolf checked in with Kali from afar. He concluded she knew he had detached himself from her, and her energy was going to change. Since they traveled for so long together. Mywolf felt an empty part in his chest where he had connected with Kali, as she did. Their experiences and Astral travels were a bond they could never erase, no matter how detached he was from her. The unseen as Mywolf was, existed just a breath away in reality. Mywolf now could travel back and forth and go into her life. There will be moments for him to check in on her. He wanted her to always feel Safe and Happy.

Kali swirled around to look behind. She sensed someone. She could sense a presence, but no one was there. A thought came into her mind to visualize her waterfall. She did and felt calmer. There was nothing to fear. She felt Safe. With her journal out, she released whatever needed to be let go of with her favorite tool of taking pen to paper. She felt off but was clueless; why?

"Perfection

You wait for me to acknowledge you daily!
To glance out beyond the walls of this home that sits upon your magnificence.
Sometimes, I do; other times, I get too busy.
It is the hustle and bustle of life that takes me away from the elegance of your Sight.

Today, the glowing flow of your water made my heart skip a beat.

Your vastness, calmness, and serenity allow your essence to nurture me.
Even when you are angry, I recognize you are cleansing yourself of debris.
It saddens my soul to see your sorrow.
All the abuse you endure for many.
For the clueless here!
Today, I am Blessed because of you.

When God created you, it was for sustenance, love, light, and vision.
A home for all of humanity!
Still, many humans trash you, violate you, and disregard your purpose.
It is you that gives us Life.
Perfection could be your title.
But we call you mother.

It is your Nature to take Life in stride as we abuse you.
Today, I am Honored to Live with you.

I cringe to guess what life could become without you.
I Worship you for many things, but mostly for the Gifts you offer;
Your Foundation, the Earth Connects all, as One!
The Waters that Flow give us a Choice, to go with the Flow of Life.
The Fire that warms us from the Sky beckons to us to become Aware.
The Air you offer Connects us to Breathe daily to Exist.

Today, I Cherish that I am Witness to you.
Your Grace is beyond;
The land, trees, waters, birds, fish, animals, plants, sun, stars, moon, and sky
so blue
Which blankets us with everything we ever need!

You are the Universe that many refuse to See.
I am in awe of your Belief in us that we can change and be set free—
That we can Respect this Planet that you offer in this Life Experience, we Share
by an Act that shows we Care.

Today, I say thank you!
For guiding us to start Anew!"

Kali looked at her paper and wondered where these deep thoughts came from when she began to write. Kali felt as if another wrote them. She knew she held the pen, but it was not her writing.

As she imagined, an essence was controlling her mind and pen. Kali was being told information. Her thoughts were of another. Who was this other? In her heart, she knew it was not Mywolf. There was a Magical/Mystical/Mystery atmosphere around her as if someone dropped stardust onto her. She felt as if she could float if she needed to reach the sky.

Composing, in her journal, always settled her. After rereading her words, she felt fragile. Vulnerable? Kali stretched her body and took a moment to center herself, light Incense, and say a Prayer to Connect her to Spirit. Her thoughts in her head were not hers. There was a Knowing she was being guided forward on a Mission. She was clueless as to the details of this Mission. Her life was getting complicated and surreal. Time to meditate, so she sat in her chair and closed her eyes.

Chapter Seventeen
The Magic/Mystery of One's Truth

Mywolf watched as Kali played with the thoughts in her Mind. Change was Growth. Growth was Expansion of Self. Expansion of Self was Ascension. Ascension was Love. Love was Unity for Life. Kali was ready now to Channel and Collaborate and Partner with the Unseen and Connect to the Ancient Wisdom of Life. The many different points on her journey have supported her by different energies experienced. One needs to be aware and consistent in life, Mywolf Imagined. Kali was such a person!

Within her Heart, Soul, and Spirit, Kali formed an escape at a young age from the pain to travel into her Safe Place of Peace. She ached for the Return to Self and her True Home. There had always been an underlying belief there was *"more"* to this life she lived daily. Kali wanted *"more,"* and in doing so, she has developed her plan to teach that this communication is possible. The biggest *"ahh moment"* for Kali was trying to understand at a very young age the simple answer to: *"Why were people not kind?"*

Mywolf imagined that this Illusion in Life that all Life is Real as is has played a game that is of a lower Belief in humans. The Memory that rests within for *"more"* is a Truth of Self, that many negate. Death is the greatest example that there is *"more!"* Karma is the little inkling that surfaces in situations with a feeling that I've done this before. At that moment is the moment of Truth for humans to grasp and ponder. To actually stop and ask themselves, *"What am I feeling at this moment?"*

It has been a journey of Insight, Guidance, Clarity, and Discovery for Kali because of the simple fact that she is a Seeker of Life and *"the all that is!"* The Mind is a powerful tool, Mywolf believed, but the use of this tool requires an

Open Heart and Belief in Love. It takes humans a long time to develop such a tool and Belief.

It has been a deep Discovery of Self for Kali to now teach it is possible to acknowledge the power of the Mind by focusing on developing an Open Heart with Love of Self to Manifest the Temples within to Open their doors through the codes of the written word that are available to all.

Part Two
Connecting to Elemental Truth

Introduction
Mywolf Exits Violet Enters

As Mywolf exits the world of Kali, her world opens to the magnificent communication from Violet her Dragon, Spirit Guide of the unseen world.

It is a journey that begins In Part Two with Day 1 to Day 222 of insight, guidance, and clarity for Kali...

Kali will now open her mind and heart to hear answers to her many questions from her Dragon Spirit Guide Violet. She sensed Violet's voice in her mind and is open to receive any information that Kali desires to know.

A daily guidance starting in September Kali is aware that Mywolf is no longer with her and that she has Violet to communicate with for now. The month's, titled September 2018 to July 2019 offers a look for those to journey with Kali and Violet from the unseen world as part of life for all to open to.

Kali looks around her home and is witness to the many Totem Animals she has collected throughout her life. She smiles because she was never aware that they helped her and led her to meeting others.

And, now the truth of life begins for all to open up to the elemental world for insight, clarity, and guidance in their life experience ...

Kali knew of the essence of the elemental world for a very long time. Knowing time is of the human mind, she realized life was not as it seemed. She lay in bed, imagining life differently compared to the years she has lived. Not of a person being a human but a person being a Spirit! Her truth lay in the foundation that there is an inner passion of belief. She was a spiritual being experiencing a human existence.

Her search for freedom was not from her parents, husband, or children but from that which she termed humanity. The veil, ever so thin, became nourishment for her to wander toward when the human part of life was too challenging. Angels, Ascended Masters, totem animals were her friends as long as she could remember. She prayed to them, spoke to them, and asked them for guidance and protection. It was a fierce belief that she was never alone. She belonged to the unseen world of heaven and beyond in her mind's eye.

It was a path she walked for many lifetimes she imagined today. She had such characteristic reminders she had done something she was doing in the present that was from a very long time ago. When she wrote in her journal, she felt she was in a cave and, as a seer, was keeping a record of facts for the future. Another time not desiring to travel outside her home, she believed she was still a monk and needed to stay safe in the comfort of her home. There were moments where she would travel in meditation to a time and place, not of today's world or surroundings. These were the seconds, quick reflections that popped into her mind as if she was not of this world. Then she would wonder, what world am I part of?

Kali traveled back to the years or maybe lifetimes with Mywolf. She felt his energy around her today but knew there was no longer a need for his guidance in her life. A small voice continued to whisper to her now, which she was not familiar with. Kali was on a journey of discovering the elemental, spiritual world of the reality of her freedom.

In her heart, she waited for the Key to unlock her truth of self. A truth that was the awakening of her Spirit-Self to its fullness. A slight smile crossed her lips, and she closed her eyes to meditate. Her greatest moments were when she looked within and connected to her light. A simple sentence in her mind would raise her memories to connect to the Light within.

Clueless for a long time what this was in the past, she now knew it was that Light within that everyone on planet earth owned. We are all born from Spirit. Spirit of Self is the Light within. All humans are given *"free will"* to experience life while Awakening to their Spirituality. When the connection to their inner Light turns on, Freedom is the reward. Most humans search for Freedom, which cannot be discovered as a human. Kali now knows Freedom is through the Spiritual aspect of Self. It is an inner calling that whispers ever so gently within the Light of Self to become Aware.

Connecting to this essence of the unseen part of the Self is the discovery of the unseen world of elementals. Kali summoned within the reflection of her journey that fueled her Soul. The books consumed as nourishment as if she was starving and would die if she did not devour them immediately. The alternative beliefs that owned her mind daily. She was so far out of the box of life, she felt she could fly on her own.

Recently, Rainbows and swirling Light filled her mind's eye. She was clueless about why or what was being downloaded. Her daily practices of Prayer, Meditation, and Writing in her journal, along with her Rituals of Incense, Candles, Aromatherapy, and Affirmations comforted her. It was this ability she possessed to stay True to that which filled her with Joy and Connection of some kind to Believe and know in the *"more"* of Life!

There was a stirring within that Change was once again upon her. The path was Changing and Manifesting her deepest dreams in Life. Communicating with an Unseen Being was a priority for her to Create. A sort of Passion of Belief that the Magic/Mystical/Mystery existence of Life waited for all to Embrace. Just as she knew of all the totem animals in Life that helped her in challenging times, she knew of another coming forward now.

There seemed to be a Fire in her Heart she could not put out. Closing her eyes, she settled into a deep Meditation and met Violet. Violet had her back, was the Fire that was stirring, and her Dragon Spirit Guide. There would be a Communication, Collaboration, Partnership, and a Channeling between them in a special journal she had to go purchase with a Dragon Symbol on its cover.

Kali heard in her thoughts so clearly, this voice of Violet. She knew it was part of her journey to walk her path now with Violet to discover a Map that needed to be shared in life with humanity. It was a Truth of Life that all had the ability to experience when they used the Key within that all possessed.

Once journal and pen were in hand, Kali sat down, lighted a piece of Incense, and asked questions to get Insight, Clarity, Communication, and Guidance from Violet. This was the beginning of a daily routine that would Inspire and offer Information to Kali to Share with humanity. Kali followed the voice within to begin this new Ritual of Channeling from her Dragon Spirit Guide Violet. In doing so, she realized this was the reason that Mywolf was no longer around her and that he had stepped away to allow Violet entrance.

The craziest part of this Collaboration was that it felt natural to Kali. For the longest of times, Kali has never felt alone, has never been bored. Her life was words, paper, pen, reading, and writing. In reflection, she wondered about the world she lived in since a small child of ten. One evening while gazing out her window and looking up at the stars, she knew there was a bigger part to live. She had felt it that night in her entire being. However, at such a young age, she was not Aware of the Journey that lied ahead in Life for her. The challenges and the Choice to be Love in all situations that filled her with fear.

Today she felt no fear. She felt Accepted into a part of Life that would help her to be of Service to Humanity in the form of Sharing information that she was given. Kali was ready! It always amazed her how she just Accepted a way of living in life daily through Ritual and Knowing of the basis of being able to travel across the Veil that was a breath away from her. It filled her with a deep inner Knowing of Love for Life that she truly wanted to Share. Kali was Aware that there were many who would not be open to her way of believing. But, she Imagined, maybe just maybe there is a Reason for this Channeling that will Open the Minds and Hearts of Humanity to travel alongside her, to learn of the *"more"* of life.

"There I go again," she whispers to herself, stepping outside the box of normalcy but yet feeling normal. She wrote on the cover of her new journal:

Violet, My Spirit Guide… The Beginning!

MYWOLF

Mywolf followed Kali's thoughts from far away now. Proud he was of her openness to receive insight, clarity and guidance to the many questions she possessed from the world of dragons! Mywolf was aware of Kali's inner thoughts and how open she has always been to the magic of life. There was no mystery just a deep knowing that there was more.

The Beginning!
Channeling Violet
My Dragon Spirit Guide

Day 1, September 20, 2018

Kali began with an acknowledgment... *My Beloved Violet, thank you for coming into my life at this time as a Dragon Spirit Guide for me. I am very humbled by this experience. I hear you. I feel you. I see you. What is your plan for me to follow?*

Violet's Voice Whispered in Her Mind as She Took the Dictation...

Our plan together as we begin our collaboration shall be daily, Kali. We will meet, and you will channel me. I shall guide you forward. It is I that is the guide for you for this lifetime. It is my fire you ignite to those who are ignorant of your truth. Your love amazes me beyond, but then I see this same love and commitment in your daughters. A brave woman is not so simple to be during chaos and confrontation, and yet you have done well. Yes, I have your back and have been the strength for you to carry always. You can ask me anything. You can call on me anytime. I will inspire you with speech and words written. I am Violet, your Dragon Spirit Guide!

Day 2

Violet, would you like to come into my day with me?

Delighted I am to join and be of service to you, Kali. Many have much fear and pain and choose to stay in it. Many refused to love themselves, but miracles happen. We will work together to heal the fears and pain. Your open heart and love confuse many, for they have never experienced it so completely since their own childhoods. You offer to see others truly, to hear them, and this is a great gift you possess.

Thank you, Violet, for your insight! I look forward to our communications. I am thrilled to have someone to speak to. How often will we channel?

You will know! When the book is full, you will not need to write anymore, unless you so desire. I love this book! Thank You!

Day 3

I am here as instructed, Violet. Speak to me and guide me this day. I am humbled to have this time with you.

We are a team and good together. I am happy to guide and inspire you. Writing is a gift I enjoy, and I am filled with words to share. We will write lots of things. You will travel a new path now, so stay open to hear me as you have been doing. I see your concern for nature and life, that is, as you say, "Here on earth, before us."

It is an interesting human you live with. So fearful and guarded. His wounds are deep from many lifetimes. He had a choice with you, but his ego roars too loud for him to hear you. Many times, you have struggled, but you always choose love as a blessing in disguise gifted from Spirit. Is it love for him? Yes, it is and love for self. This lifetime I honor you because of your connection to Spirit and nature. As we are one, know now how powerful you are in what you know. It matters not but that you grow and expand to help humanity heal with Spirit, with "Me," Violet, Your Dragon Spirit Guide, who has waited to begin.

Day 4 (Into the Woods...)

Kali is surprised as she reflects on the day. Violet has come into my mind's eye at the waterfall!

Thank you for letting me see how beautiful a dragon you are. I feel I am in slow motion this day. Yet, here I sit, waiting to receive a message. I am very new to this. I do have great patience. As I now communicate with Violet, I am humbled but so happy. I had asked for this for a long time. I feel blessed to achieve all that I do. With love, light, and joy in my heart, I am very grateful, Violet!

Sitting here in meditation, two spirits had the following message for me about the woods that surround me: "Rake the dead out of the woods!" My beautiful willow tree said, "Get the dead branches off of me!" She also told me that I am loved by nature beings because I love nature! Willow filled my palms with grounding earth energy! Violet, I could sense elementals around me now, but I could not see them. I felt that when the trees moved in the wind, it is a form of greeting for me. I could hear them clearly!

Kali realized that she had taken Violet's Journal with her into the woods and felt that she had upset Violet. In the woods, it was the world of the elementals that spoke to Kali in the form of a communication and partnership she was developing.

She continued... I am new at this, Violet, and I really don't know what I can and cannot ask of you. I do realize I can invite you into my day and writing sessions. What else? How do I know it is you I am communicating with?

You are not in slow motion, for everything is at divine timing always. Our pattern of collaboration will be daily wherever you are at the time. Feel your body sensation that changes and know this is me, Violet. I know that you felt upset about taking my journal, and the reason was that you were looking to communicate with elementals. I am not an elemental per se but really a Spirit Guide for you. It matters not because you realized too late about the journal. This is my journal where only you and I need to communicate. You can ask anything. All that you know is true so far.

We will both get better at this as I observe the challenges you face. You do well to call out to me whenever you need answers. I see that you are very adaptable. I am your guide for life challenges, healing, information that only you require to helping yourself and help humanity.

Quickly you caught on when the tree spirits spoke to you. All will combine in time. We have lots of work to do together. Ask me anything?

Can I open the Akashic Records with seven questions for people? If this works for you? You must use all that you have learned, adapted to what works for you. If it works, use it!

Will you be inspiring me on my blog topics? Who do you think inspired you always, especially when it comes to information that people can relate to and benefit from?

You ask questions you know the answer to. If you believe something, know it is the truth. You are powerful, and your thoughts that come and go are reflections on what you truly know. I will help you with anything you ask me to help you with.

We are working in secret to an extent because people do not relate to life as you do.

Day 5

Violet, I have many questions for you.

Questions are filling your mind! Begin, Kali…

- *How can I know it is you I am receiving information from?*
- *Are you a healing dragon?*
- *Do you want to join with me and guide me when I speak with people?*
- *Are you my main guide at this time?*
- *Has it been you guiding me toward the Akashic Records Readings?*
- *Are you happy about the dragon skull I purchased?*

I will try to answer all of your questions. Feel me in your heart. I am a Dragon that protects and heals. Yes, I do! I also work with the elemental realm. You are to use all your tools. Just stay focused on what you can do and need to do. I like the picture of the female Dragon you possess in your healing room.

Day 6

Violet, I feel that at this time, you have a message for me? Earlier I received the thought that you wanted me to channel you daily, to get a book on Dragons and buy the necklace that matches the print I bought?

Yes! Yes! Yes! All is true from me to you to answer your insights. I have much teaching to share with you. You are on fire now, and I am here as your Dragon Spirit Guide to answer your questions. You have many! It seems you follow directions well, fast, and accurate in thoughts you receive. It will not take you long to prosper on your path. We, myself, and the elemental realm are here for you. Just think about us, and we will hear you. Never think it is not me answering you unless you are in the woods. As your guide, I will always have your back. I laughed at you wanting to wear my name. If it pleases you, get a "V." LOL, as you say.

Educate yourself on the world of Dragons. I am a Fire Dragon, as you asked earlier. You are ready for me to be of service so you can be of service to others. We are a good team. I am happy if you are happy and you are very eager. Very ready to learn.

Your teachers are all around you. Do what you will to show others the way. At times you let slip by the information you can share that you will benefit from as well as another. I do know your thoughts, as you hear mine. Stay tuned into me, and we will progress daily to all that will fulfill your purpose. Stay focused and do that, which is your passion and purpose before anything else.

There are many hours to do it all. Just stay on your path, and the journey will be magical with me and you communicating daily. Just like a time for meditation. You need a time with me to run things over with me as I am your guide. You asked for a guide. I am here, so consistency from you is a requirement of our partnership.

I am grateful that you listen so well and pay attention most of the time to your thoughts. This is extremely necessary for your expansion and opening to all your intuitive abilities.

Day 7

Good Morning, Violet I am ready to hear from you and channel your message. At times, I feel you around me and smile. I looked into getting a book, necklace, and Fire Dragons, too. Thank you for inspiring me...

I know of all and excited that you are aware when I am around you. There are small ways to check in with you. I am preparing you for bigger ways in the future. The time will come when hours of your time will be needed as part of your participation. Videos are nothing compared to what will be expected of you. Your diet is superb, continue on this path. Educate yourself about all that I can help you with, for it will save me time. There are many words you will use daily that will surprise you. But, just go with the flow. I need books on our journey to be shared, so write, write, write, it all down.

The time is not yet, but within the new year, great change will be upon you, and you will receive support, inspiration, and guidance. You are finally exactly where you have always been meant to be. I am your Fire Dragon Spirit Guide, and I have waited to be known by you. It was a journey to get you to this page. Daily we will meet, and I will walk with you always.

Day 8

My dear Violet, I apologize for this late communication with you, but you came into my thoughts, and I knew I had to be with you, as you said daily. I thank you!

You have had an interesting day, which you struggle with because you enjoy the Spirit world. Yet, as you tell yourself, you live in a human world and must be part of it! I see you spoke of me this day. You are fearless. Your granddaughter needs to be led to believe the Unicorns and Dragons are real but on a different dimension. Keep that door open for her as much as you can.

I know of all that you desire but one step at a time, one day at a time. Much needs to be focused on and given light to so go with the flow of your thoughts, listen, and be aware. Keep a "to-do" book. Write all that comes into your thoughts down. This is your journey to do as we get to know one another.

I am delighted that you are so eager and open to the Spirit world. You are more adaptable to us in the woods. But just being outdoors helps us communicate with you most of the time. Walk out-of-doors as you do in the woods.

MYWOLF

Mywolf decided to check in on Kali. He felt in his heart that this is a new way of communicating for her with Violet. As he is not allowed to let her feel his essence so she can stay connected to Violet daily, he quickly looked in on her to see how she was processing everything. The path of humans was to handle and receive just as much as they can from the unseen world of spirit when the time was right. There was no need for overload.

Chapter Eighteen
October 2018

Day 9

Good afternoon, Violet; I know that there is a reason for everything in life! Can you explain this day to me?

Go slowly toward your dreams. Process and digest your thoughts and ideas. No jumping in first! You will get overwhelmed. There is much coming to do, to learn, and to achieve. Write, blog, and get back to our book, "A Key to the Unseen World." Navigate a map of sorts of what to focus on daily.

Consistency is always necessary to achieve mastery. They will consider you a master in your field, so breathe, process, digest, and take it slow. Responsibility comes to self, so you can help another. To help another, you must focus and enjoy doing all that you do.

Day 10

Good afternoon, Violet! How are you? How am I doing? Can I tell people about you?

I am enjoying you, and you are doing wonderfully. You can tell people you have a guide named Violet that is working with you for now. Many are not ready for dragons and such. Ha-Ha-Ha! Tell those who believe as you do when you feel they understand. Know you hear well and follow directions. You are eager and a true teacher.

I like your way of writing. You jump right in, and you never hesitate. As an old soul, you have done many of what you are passionate about before. Know we are honored as beings of the unseen world to work and partner with you. Show us what you desire and need, so we will help you. Otherwise, we will take the lead. We are many, so be open to it all.

You have noticed that you can now receive information from another's Higher Self to your Higher Self. This is powerful. It is not me but the connection you personally are now manifesting. Stay true to your soul's desires, and all will unfold quickly. You are open to Spirit's different forms.

Day 11

Good evening, Violet! How are we doing?

Processing is now in progress; moving, resting, and water are essential. Be true to yourself and all you desire now. The grand babies need your love and light. You bring joy to them. In the next few days, your vision of life will expand. Be open to all as it is your journey and will be of help to you in many ways. Ask anything of me. I am here for you at all times.

This desire to be alone and with Spirit is because you are moving fast to be the truth of your purpose and passion. The life that is required of you as a human stops you and feels like a waste of time. This is not so. As a human, your love and light help wherever you go with whoever you are with. It is a process. A part of being human! Many love you, and you never know who you are healing just by spending time with them. This is the beauty of Spirit connection.

Continuously doing the best you can be. Rest yourself when you need to. It is a blessing for me to guide you now. Opening further to insight is to be, eventually. However, you are perceptive and capable of always seeing the truth in situations. Doubt none of this. It is true. It is real. It is the process of intuition and insight to believe it as you receive it.

Unfortunately, for you, the change that will come has to come only because it is time for us to share your mastery. Un-cord yourself from those that do not serve your highest good. Stay true to Spirit in all situations now.

Day 12

Good morning, Violet; can you help me with all that I am desiring to learn now? And why?

Spirit takes you to the teachers that can empower and expand your awareness of life with Spirit.

You will experience an awakening of inner wisdom and how to teach what you have learned. Price is a choice to the one who wants to teach and the one who wants to learn. You can help one another. Your experience is different as others are to them. Yes, there is a reason for all situations, as you are aware. Time will tell how this will switch.

Let others know what you know. To be certified is important for many, but you know it matters not. Be brave. Be wise. Be truthful. Share your thoughts with others as they are also discovering what they are to share with the world.

Never think you are less. You are equal. You are a teacher of Spiritual Tools to empower and heal humanity. Go for it!

Day 13

Good morning, Violet! Congratulations on Dragon Day! What does this mean? I am at the home by the waterfall. What do you feel is the reason that this property is in my life?

Thank you for congratulating us Dragons! Today, Dragons celebrate and honor one another's gifts and abilities in helping humankind. There are many Spirit Dragon Guides that protect and guide those with potential for mastery as you are. I feel blessed to travel your journey and see the joy you receive from Gaia. She is grateful for your love, respect, and support. When you travel into the woods, now has a purpose. This land you are at is special for many faeries. The water is to be blessed with love and honored by you because it nourishes many.

This is a lifetime of living for generations to come. It is in your life as a remembrance of the simplicity of life, and how the less you have, the happier you truly are. The less you eat, the happier and longer you live. Simplicity is a deep desire of yours. Simplicity, you shall have. All that is not of Gaia, not of Spirit, is useless. There is no struggle when one lives in Spirit with simplicity. Life is better, and one's health as well is better.

Day 14

Good morning, Violet! How do I handle this situation with learning with another now? There is so much I have learned prior to now, and yet I crave more! Why?

You are struggling with a decision you made to further yourself with new learning abilities with Spirit. Honesty is best with all, for in the future, you will join with others as teachers. You can be of service to others. You have learned much more than you have realized yourself. It is a matter of refreshing yourself now. Share us all with others.

You have named me well. I refer to you as my love, my light. It blesses us to have been open to this relationship as a team.

Day 15

Dear Violet, I am very honored to communicate with you. At times during the day, I feel your presence around me. I feel protected by you during stressful moments, especially in the heavy fog last night.

Life is about handling the moments that scare you. You did well to call out to me during the heavy fog. I know of you the instant you call out. Remember, I have your back. You desire to learn Quantum Healing, which will help many but is really not needed. You heal. We all heal. Allow it all to happen, and it will.

Incorporation of other's teachings will be a benefit in different ways for you in the future.

Day 16

Good morning, Violet! How am I doing? Are my beliefs and thoughts correct on all that I am writing, reading, typing, and imagining? Do you have a means for me to communicate with you through thought where at the moment I ask, and you will answer? Is there a sign that you can give me that it is you?

A sign you ask for: the color violet, tingling sensation, and it is me right by your side. At times you doubt, and this is true of most humans, not to believe what they know. Be certain it is all so, and it is. There is no hidden agenda.

You are on target, and now you have true guides to partner and communicate with. Be certain it is so, and it is so. There is love in partnership. Trust in the love of all that you are doing for you are a being of light that is sharing the love. Love is what all of this is about. This is certain.

Love. Love. Love.

Day 17

Good morning, Violet! Why am I a wreck? What is going on with my body this morning? Help me today! Please!

Stress has taken its toll today. Doubts fill your mind. Others blast negativity at you. It is wise to ground yourself this day. Relax, and I will be at your side. There is no reason to drive yourself crazy. You can do this. Being you is to be your greatest gift to share with others. There is no fear, only this attachment you have around what you know or do not know. Trust you know, and it will surface when needed.

Setting yourself up as a teacher is work only because you trust the familiar space of yours. It is time to walk forward out into the world now. Go with love in your heart, mind, voice, and touch. Light is always brightest because of LOVE that fills it up. You are Light. Fill yourself up with LOVE no matter what.

Day 18

Good morning, Violet! What can you tell me about this process of communicating with you daily? What can I expect in doing this?

You desire to know the process with me and what you can expect?

I am always with you. Call on me for help in all situations. Show me what I can do for you. Ask, and I will answer. We are now partners as I have come here to guide you as your Dragon Spirit Guide.

Find a book to read on Dragon Spirit Guides, so you know all I am capable of. I am with you now. Violet is the color that awakens around you as a sign as my name, it is so.

Day 19

Good morning, Violet! Are you one of the Dragons of the New Earth Consciousness? What can I do as part of this new being of consciousness?

There is power in knowing there is to be a new earth and being of consciousness for all on Gaia for Gaia to survive. You are aware. I have chosen you so I can inspire, guide, and offer you clarity. It is to be a teaching we will create together.

There is too much fear on earth. This fear is affecting Gaia as she cleanses herself of it, as well. A love we are. All are of Love. Light has to be shone on humanity for the love to surface.

The love in many is buried deep under the fear of lifetimes of struggle, anger, and hate. This can no longer be part of this world's consciousness to move up to 5th dimensional. Even if it only reaches a few, it is to be a process toward change, growth, and expansion.

Be Light. Be Love. There is nothing as powerful to share. Never doubt all that you know. Believe in it, no matter how different it is from another's beliefs. Each has a journey of their own to walk. Walk your path with Light and Love.

Day 20

Good morning, Violet! Am I on the right track with these thoughts about energy healing?

You pay attention and listen well. It was I who started this morning with you. The belief that more is on its way for you, but an action needs to be taken. Get yourself visible. Sharing and teaching are what a being of service is all about.

You are on track. You straddle two worlds. Yes, Yes, Yes! But, stay present in your world because that is where you are needed.

Truly you are blessed to know of the Spirit world daily through partnership and communication. This is beautiful. All is happening as planned with us. I feel honored to be of service.

Day 21

Good afternoon, Violet! I am processing information that comes to me. Is all this information coming from you?

Most of your inner guidance comes from me to get you into the practice of communicating with me and receiving it. I am business, counseling, writing, sessions all the information to inspire and guide you. I am here as your Dragon Spirit Guide. I Guide and Protect!

Thank you, Violet. I also thank you for better sleep and a remembrance of my dreams!

You are welcome! Rest when you need to!

Day 22

Good morning, Violet! There were three words I was awakened with, and I cannot remember them. Can you help me with them? What did these words mean?

Type up my guidance! Call it, Violet, My Dragon Spirit Guide! Spiritualized Teaching is to be your mantra! As a Spirit of Love and wisdom to be, be a light for those in darkness. It is your path to help humanity to look for the Light in their lives. It is what you have achieved.

Teach all that you released that no longer served you. You have risen out of darkness and out of fear. The Light suits you much better. Share and teach the process with a touch of Spirit in a membership. Do not struggle with your thoughts. It is simple, teach what you know.

Teach the choices you created in your life step by step. No one grows and expands overnight. It is a process. Teach this process to others, and you will succeed on your path, as well.

Day 23

Good morning, Violet! Woke up, I think around 4 am, fell back asleep around 5 am or 7 am. Feel a bit groggy now. Why does this happen at this time?

When you awake around 4 am, this is a chance for you to meditate, to go within at the earliest of the hour that the veil is thinnest. It is a benefit to your journey. You do well to meditate and take it as a time to pray. Superb for you to continue doing so if something awakens you at this hour. Just know there is a reason or everything.

The path is set to move forward. To teach all that you know. You asked for more, and I will give it, but I wonder why all that you have studied is not enough. Is it curiosity like the Cheshire cat or a need to fulfill a thought of your own that haunts you?

Be certain of your choices; curiosity killed the cat.

Day 24

Good morning, Violet! Thank you for your words of love and insight during the day.

As a human, you are fast. Fast is the path you choose sometimes. Too quickly, but you can see the entire picture. Being honest and true is a gift you own. You are open to the unseen world. You are opening as well to getting things done. Being eager to learn can help you or harm you. Still, there are no mistakes, only that which fills you with a passion to share and offer with love.

Yours is to heal through word and energy, and you have the foundation and tools already. Anything else that you desire will arrive on time for you to use. As fast as you can be, you have patience. You can only follow your heart and what speaks to you is what you desire to teach to heal humanity.

This is huge.

Day 25

Good morning, Violet! How can I know when I am actually channeling Spirit, you, and any other guides of mine?

You will know who you are channeling because it is in the language. We speak differently from you and different from one another. Go into your heart and sense and even ask us who we are.

You can only be you. You can only choose yourself to change, and you have done so.

All have had many warnings and times to choose another way. Many punish themselves daily by their choices of yesterday and today.

Day 26

Good morning, Violet! How can you help me to process my session from yesterday with quantum healing?

In helping you to process information you receive from a quantum healing session, once again, know what you know. Your insight and intuition are spot on.

Like is like. Dark is dark. Light is light. The personality has not changed as you can bear witness to. This is now between the soul and the personality to become whole in all humanity at times.

Fear is powerful and fuels pain, sickness, and death. Before this switch, the personality was dark, and did not desire to be here. What does this personality now say? All the same things!

Within, the demons, a battle exists. Soul to soul is how you need to communicate to survive the time. Be you! Just be as you have been! No change is necessary from you.

Your life will be the same afterward as it is now. Especially if you desire to travel. Again, that would be your greatest discovery of self. Know there is truth in all you do. Be true to your beliefs, for these are the lessons you chose and will be of great benefit in teaching the truth of self.

Day 27

Good morning, Violet! At times, I procrastinate! Why?

You are struggling with all that is desired of you, but you are capable. Just be you and have fun doing what you do at all times. Life is busy. You are busy. Time is of no relevance so do what fuels you passionately.

Rest when you need to. Go for a walk. You can only do what excites, invigorates, and fills you with joy. You are extremely connected to your beliefs around life. Being focused is required to getting things done. Do only what you want to do at all times. There is a tremendous change coming your way. Be ready in body, mind, and spirit to process and digest it all.

Your vibration is changing. Take it easy this day. Read, rest if you feel tired. Sleep even if needed. Your mind is opening to *"the all that is,"* and you may feel dizzy. Close your eyes and breathe.

Day 28

Good evening, Violet! I am drained! Why?

The draining you ask about is a cleaning up of your field. Life troubles your soul. It is the beliefs of others that scare your soul. You are a being of light, and that is all you need to concern yourself with. You have the gift to see another way and to believe differently because you lack fear. Many are filled with fear.

You are very blessed to have grasped a true belief that love is all there is. Yours is a life to be challenged by all that you hold dear and believe is not like others. Stay focused on your dreams and all that connects you to the light within, for that is a great tool to own.

The energy of fear drains you, but it is not yours, so rest and nourish yourself with all that you have. This is your power. Breathe. Step back. Ground yourself and stay true to your beliefs.

It has been a long day to reflect on other people's choices, that is the gift of *"free will."* Choose yours, which is of love, and let others choose theirs.

Day 29

Good morning, Violet! What is going on with me? I feel weird.

You say you feel weird, and you want to know what is going on? A shift is taking place. A release of all that no longer serves you. This is a process of peeling the onion, as you say. It is a cleansing of yesterday, even many past lifetimes. Humans like yourself get attached to lots of debris in your field from each other. To open to Spirit totally, the debris has to be cleansed.

You are now in this process of removal to become a pure being to connect to Spirit.

The Spirit world is watching and helping you process this release. Be gentle with yourself, rest, walk, or sit outside to receive energy from Spirit. Open to this change, and your life will unfold quickly to do all that your soul, as Spirit teaches.

It is a process of manifestation unique to you.

Day 30

Good morning, Violet! I have floaters in my eyes that cloud my sight, and at times I cannot see. Why is this? Can I heal this?

You have trouble seeing. Your thoughts brought this to manifest. It is from your subconscious beliefs from yesterday. Open your heart to all, see all with love, and know just like you have *"free will"* and desire to be you; they do too. They may question your choices as you question their choices. This is to be cleansed. Let them choose for themselves.

There is no control in the world of Spirit, only love. Think as a Spirit now in all situations, and you will see a difference. Open to this path of Spirit to clearly manifest your journey.

- No questions about another's choices.
- No doubt why someone is in your life.
- Spirit cannot make mistakes, only human minded detached from Spirit believe there are mistakes in life.
- Now start your journey of truth as Spirit.
- See as Spirit. Hear as Spirit. Speak as Spirit. Love as Spirit.
- This is your choice to do so, and now it begins.

Day 31

Good morning, Violet; there are many thoughts filling my mind about this amazing journey I am discovering as I open to Source and channeling. Is this the process?

Kali, you desire to know the process and all that swirls around in your mind. The process is a belief in all that you are led to. The process is opening to Source further. The process is consistency and focus, sprinkled with dedication and passion. It is a journey you have chosen and one you are superb at. There is always the thoughts and questions of the human to fill you up. You are fantastic at going with the flow, so just flow.

I am your Dragon Spirit Guide, and I am exactly here to guide you. This door of communication has opened, and we must now communicate by you channeling. It is a great gift you have, this love for the written word. It flows well with you.

It is a true passion as a scribe for many lifetimes. A deep fascination from the past, writing, words, and all that goes with being a writer. It is a part of your purpose in life and a way of sharing information. Words can heal and harm. Positive truth and words of love are a truth you are well versed in sharing as a writer.

Day 32

Good morning, Violet; what am I to believe about information that I sense is not on point?

You ask questions you already know the answers to, Kali. So, here is insight; trust you know. This is a teaching for you to gain a belief in yourself. Others do not know as you do. Verification was the act of your insight into the belief system you have gained. Love of life is a journey of the process of insight, belief, and that you can only consider as truth. The greatest lesson for you is that you know. Believe it is so, and act accordingly.

You do not need permission when you choose love as an action. It is the oneness of the journey that allows healing for you, for others, and stretches out to *"the all that is."*

- Change and growth are the first steps of raising your vibration.
- Consistency and belief are the second steps.
- Transformation and Love for all are the third steps.

It is a process, one step in front of the other as a human walking this Spiritual path of connection, collaboration, and partnership with the realm of a Spirit-guided existence in becoming wholeness.

Day 33

Good morning, Violet; what is going on this day? I feel off, in a funk again. Why?

You question the changes you are feeling from the depths within. It is an unfoldment of the journey before now. There is much despair from your past that is being processed. Kali, always listen to your inner guidance and know as you know the truth of self. Opening your eyes to all that you need personally to release is a process as well, that only you can choose.

There is much desire and passion you own to share. However, how you believe, many do not. Tread lightly on this path as you open to the world of channeling Spirit. It is an opening of Self to be pure as a channel. Do not attach yourself to an outcome. For all will come in due time. You are here! I am here!

Being open to teachings from another is part of the unveiling of all that you need now to experience. Remember, Spirit is truth, but you are experiencing the human equivalent that is pure only to you. No one else can know you or do as you do, as the Spirit/Human you are, choosing to be of service to humanity. Ease and grace are the opening to a fulfilled journey on the path of your choice to be of service as a healer. You are a healer beyond what you imagine, in thought, word, and action.

Day 34

Good morning, Violet; I believe you are guiding me to read certain books at this time. Is this true?

You have tuned in to me and have heard books that will inform you on this journey of the unseen world. Yes, it is to be so, I am the one whispering in your ear. It is the teachings needed for you to enjoy. Change is upon you, and you listen well. Opening to the unseen world is necessary to help raise humanity's vibration.

It is to be always a free choice, and you are open and wise to grasp the reality of wholeness by being in the human/Spirit world of Angels, Ascended Masters, and such.

Now to be in the truth of Spirit/Human Being, the world of Source as a partnership is a healing for you.

Many are not ready to communicate one-on-one; that is why you will be the outlet for Source to download wisdom to teach. You are open and aware of many who do so already, but they need more. So, it is a process you need to open to, to educate yourself on the new path you will be traveling now. It has been your choice to do so, and I have now answered your prayers. Enjoy this time of learning and discovery for change, expansion, and an opening to all is a step away.

Day 35

Good morning, Violet; I am sad about the choices of others. I know I have no control, but I am also aware I can choose how I desire to live. Have I chosen the right path now?

As you can see, your light beams out from you to allow another to choose another way. This is healing. This is a choice for the better. There is never a right or wrong way; it always comes down to a choice which many grasped onto, as fear. It is difficult for many to choose love as you do. You are certain with love, and this is a teaching.

The path of love has no fear. You listened to your body and the ache within for peace. All need peace to exist as a whole being of love. There will be no separation if there is love and inner peace. It is this calmness that will heal you and others in life. *"Free will"* is a choice given to choose, but even after choosing fear, one can choose again, and love can be the choice to heal, forgive, and be whole again. Love is the essence of wholeness when chosen in life situations.

Day 36

Good morning, Violet; I am thrilled to be able to channel you. Is there anything I am in need of focusing on to be of service this day?

You ask what you need to focus on being of service this day? The truth of this path is consistency from you. As you believe, it is an example of this as it unfolds to joining in a deep vision of wholeness. The path moves as quickly as you deem it to be. Focusing on a life of service filled with joy and happiness for all is a beginning. The vision of all that you witness is the goodness in life.

Stay in wonder and awe that all is exactly as it needs to be. It is a journey of self-discovery for all of humanity. In doing so, wholeness is possible. It takes the consistency of action, dedication, and manifestation of one's belief to walk a journey filled with the act of serving. Opening the self to the belief that nothing truly is as it seems to be.

There is vastness for the daily function of life that many are clueless of. The ego of self that craves materialistic power suffers from within because there can never be enough for the ego. Walk forward, connecting in wholeness and trust that this is the process. That which guides and inspires you, to do, to be, of service.

Day 37

Good morning, Violet; this journey is amazing, and I am very grateful for your channeling and all that we are experiencing. How is this for you?

The question today is about you channeling me and how I am affected? The journey is an opening toward a partnership for all.

It is the collaboration in wholeness that will open possibilities to unfold for humanity. It is not about me or you but more about how we can help one another. In doing so, we join forces to help humanity. There is tremendous fear growing in your country, and it is not acceptable to condemn one another's choices.

"Free will" is given to all. There is no one superior to another. It becomes a belief of the ego that one knows better, and fear develops attack and criticism. Humanity today is beyond such a belief; still, most have slipped backward as if hypnotized by a force that is not of love.

Your belief, like others, is to choose love not for special people but for all. There is a divide now that has granted a separation among many as I observe your world. Too much fear governs many to attack each other for their choices, religion, color, and yet all are given *"free will."* Love is more powerful, and this is to become a willing choice.

Day 38

Good morning, Violet; this is the day the Veil is thinnest. What do I need to do tonight?

All Hallows Eve is the dream time for many to travel into the "Veil of Spirit" and communicate as you already do. Set an intention tonight for that which you desire to be of service working within the realm of Spirit, Faery, Elementals, and myself. Ask, and you shall receive.

It is the discovery of this communication that all be of service for many. It is this journey of belief that there are powers beyond the human world that wants to be of service. This is the plan, a belief that generates partnership. It has to be a mutual collaboration of coming together for the benefit of all of humanity.

There cannot be no separation, no me and no you! We are one in Spirit as you are one in humanity. To create wholeness is the joining of Spirit and Human as a complete being of pure love. It always returns to love and the foundation of the light that needs to be shared. To be of service is to be a vehicle of light and love for self and all.

MYWOLF

The days were consistent when it came to Kali and Violet collaborating now, Mywolf thought to himself. He was amazed at how open Kali was to this experience. He could imagine her in the woods sitting and meditating by her waterfall, but now she was part of the realm of Dragons.
He wondered if she even remembered him?
Mywolf had made a plan with the Council of 'the all that is,' and there was no way he was allowed to break it without consequences. He could be a witness but he could not share in her journey as before. Distance was required because of their bond and the energy of life humans possess.

Chapter Nineteen
November 2018

Day 39

Good morning, Violet; I now have this sensation of receiving teaching downloads during the night. Is this true?

I fill your nights with words you say. Wise one that you are, it is during the night when we travel to the familiar school of lessons. It is a path of processing the wisdom from many lifetimes that needs to be remembered. Restless as it may seem to you, it is necessary to connect and be taken to the "Temples of Life." The journey is the essence of deep understanding that needs to open from within.

Many lifetimes have created many lessons that are stored in your "Akashic Records." You have a sense of this, for you have been a teacher and seer in many of these lifetimes, even a monk and other religious sources to learn from. It is the memory of belief in self. That feeling you have done this before that needs to stir the pot of wisdom to arise and be shared.

It is an opening to the belief that what happens on a whole today manifests tomorrow and tomorrow and tomorrow. This is a gift many possess but few refused to believe. Unconscious many are to their power in how they think of themselves and others. Their words sting like a bee and create pain for the self and for another. The actions chosen that are not of love stop their process dead until they change.

Day 40

Good morning, Violet; my left hand feels numb at times and stiff with pain. What is this about?

You are questioning stiffness in your hand this day. It has stirred a sort of release and processing from your past up. A memory you need to release. Open your heart with love for all the small details of life from the past. It can no longer serve you to have an attachment. Your journey is a part of unconditional love. Dig deep within your mind to let the thoughts from yesterday to dissolve and be no more. Yesterday cannot be changed, only embraced as part of the journey of lessons learned. Human beings come to earth for all different lessons. Yours have brought you to the page today.

Open yourself to always follow your truth, for it is to choose love. In doing so, love is the essence of your foundation from the past. Stay true to your beliefs today and carry them into the future. It is the journey of service you seek to heal another. *Heal yourself first to do so.* There is always a process and a reason for everything. This, you know, is a truth you adhere to, and it benefits you to do so even for yourself in situations, as you have done many times before.

Day 41

Good morning, Violet; I am going to need help this day with all these personalities that are challenging at times. Can you help me, please?

You are dealing with challenging times this day. It is my pleasure to have your back. You must be true to you. Do what you need to do to stay your truth and walk your path. Others are pulled tight and ready to burst wide open by demands of the ego. It is a constant battle they fight within that excites them to lash out at others. They are not aware that they personally can choose another way of being.

It is interesting, the need to be negative and complaining, and yet even though it is exhausting, this is their choice. As beings of love born into a life of lessons and "discovery of self," change is required for many. Few are eager to do so. Stuck in their own beliefs, it can be the simple thought of knowing one is better than another. This is not so. As 'One,' we travel in the Spirit World. Separate thoughts of belief disentangle humanity to hear the ego and nothing else that would benefit them to live a life of joy and happiness at all times. You know this. Be you, a being of light and love toward all.

Day 42

Good morning, Violet; a very busy morning. I am grateful for you being in my life. I realized that I cannot function when there is lots of distraction. Why?

Distraction and interruption have fueled your day, it seems. You wonder how can you learn to say," No?" This is to be in whatever form works for you. It matters not what another understands if it does not serve you. Do that which you are in need of to move forward to create for humanity healing. When one is of service, it is a consistency of focus that is required. "Responsibility of self" as a teacher is part of being responsible for others.

Too much chaos can manifest stress for you, but you are well-grounded in all that is required of you by others. Change is good, for growth and expansion is needed on the path you are traveling. Make fewer demands on yourself, so you go with the flow of your path. To get overwhelmed will not serve you at this time, which you know of. Speak your truth. This will enable you to live your truth.

Why waste so much time doing for those who can do for themselves? To nurture yourself first in life is essential.

Day 43

Good afternoon, Violet; change is awakening within, and I need to know the plan for my future.

The future is on your mind. Stay present doing all that you desire to create and manifest this day. This is the plan you designed while in Spirit, and you are exactly on course. Listen to your positive thoughts and words you share. Sharing is a form of teaching. Dreams do come true, as you realize now.

Still, there is always a teaching of love needed for some to grasp where they are and need to travel forward. It is a path for all to listen to their heart and own instincts. There is no right or wrong, only what is chosen in life. Everyone is blessed whether they choose either one. That is the silliness of human thought. One is not right. One is not wrong. All are lessons to be learned today, tomorrow, or another life experience.

There are those who awaken to choose another way to stop the fear from traveling forward. Fear ends once a "love of self" opens that door of one accepting a lesson learned as a breath of fresh air, finally releasing freedom because of their own *"free will"* to be a choice of this love. Life is one. Each time one heals by the act of self-love, another heals in life. One awakens here. Another awakes somewhere else.

Love is a huge part of humanity. Kali, you know the basis of "being of light," is to discover love to awaken to Spirit. Still, many nurtured their inner fears and refused to choose love. Daily you are witness to the struggle in many. It is possible to teach another to love!

Day 44

Good morning, Violet; thoughts are stirring up about the change that is coming daily. It is as if I wait for this, or at least I feel something is about to change? What is this about?

This day you question that a change is approaching?

- Change is all around you and within.
- Is it not a change of self that has taken place already?
- Do you not channel me, and open your Akashic Records now?

This is all new! Change is definitely clear in your life. That which is a greater change will come in time. Your soul knows this and is delighted to be part of this journey you have chosen. "Wholeness of self" is desired by your soul.

Remember, there is no time per se in the Spirit World, so it is a human thought in need of a deadline. You are intuitive to all in your life and feel an inner sadness for how those you love treat each other. Yet, you are open for them to find their own way in life. This is a gift few have. No control, criticism, and judgment are the greatest change for growth and "expansion of self," which you own.

Be certain all is well in life. There is a plan of choice for everyone for their thoughts, words, and actions. There is no wrong way. It is gifted to all to choose another way if they can!

Day 45

Good morning, Violet; how can I be of service to people that are not open to help themselves?

"Being of service" is on your mind this day, for people who are not open to help themselves? Just share what you feel can be of help in their lives and leave the rest to the Universe. Your knowledge is vast, and you seek to nourish yourself as many do not. Fear is the simple choice many attach to. Fear of change is the greatest in humanity's belief. Many followed as they were raised and believe it is the only way. To step out of the box can mean a betrayal of sorts to the way life has to be. Fear stops many from choosing another way.

It is the act and desire you crave to be of service that is a true blessing. One here today may grasp your message, another next time. Never stop offering teaching you know will benefit another. As a "way-shower," you can only offer them a new way of life, and the rest is up to them. This is the true basis of *"free will."* Sometimes, something will click, and miracles happen.

You know of all that is required to change today to live different from yesterday. The many hours of seeking and learning! It all is a journey of "discovery of self." Many fear the self within and refuse to seek their "truth of self" out, and it is their choice.

Day 46

Good morning, Violet; I feel blessed today to be on this "path of a discovery of self and truth." Thank you for letting me channel your guidance.

Today, you feel blessed and grateful to be a channel with me. The truth of your "discovery of self" has been journeying all along this path you chose.

Meeting your Dragon Spirit guide opens the world beyond the seen that is the truth of life. Many refused to imagine such a possibility.

Then you traveled this path seeking more and more. It was as if you needed to know and "remember for self." It is this discovery and desire that has awakened in you a "belief of self" because life is not real as it is.

Life is a place to learn to remember the "truth of self." Is that not possible for all, I ask?

Humanity has been corrupted by darkness, but *"free will"* has always been given by the Creator. Choice is *"free will"* in all of daily life.

You truly, madly, and deeply grasp this "illusion of life," and that is why you feel blessed. The opening of your mind to the unseen world that is real will allow your gifts of healing to magnify as you recall all the inner wisdom of many lifetimes. There are moments when you feel, "I have done this before!" I say to you, yes, you have for many lifetimes during challenging times. Now there are no more challenges.

Day 47

Good morning, Violet; I am loving life! I feel free of all that I experienced in my past as if I am preparing an opening for the new as a "vessel now of light." How can this be?

Kali, an opening for the new as a "vessel of light," is "true freedom" from yesterday. It is a process of integration, download, and expansion that is releasing the old for the new. Opening yourself to such teachings is the key to transformation.

You are fearless for all that no longer serves you to be omitted from your life. This is the path of a spiritual whole "being of light." The light will reflect out of your essence as a beam of the path. It is those who seek a path that will be drawn to this beam.

You shall teach all that has empowered you to say always, "IAM loving life!" It is for all to discover this essence of being born as a vessel to fill up and then release what no longer is necessary. Change is for all in life. To understand the need for change is to grow and "expand the self" to be a whole being, fearless and free.

You have given humanity a tremendous gift to cherish, for as you heal, another heals. It is this "beam of light" that is now essential for a Gaian Consciousness to allow the belief that anything is possible when one knows what fills them up is toxic and unhealthy and has to be released.

Day 48

Good morning, Violet; I am so excited to read the book, Dragons: Your Celestial Guardians, by Diana Cooper that you led me to. Now, what do I do? Do I work with these dragons in the book or just you? Do I do the exercises?

Dragons in books are part of your path of awakening. This awakening to the reality and realm of dragons is necessary for your journey. I am a Rainbow/Air/Fire Dragon when I need to be. We dragons are a family. I am your main Dragon Spirit Guide for life. It is an honor to be with such an old soul. I tried to be in your mind, but you were not ready until now.

Welcome to the Celestial Guardians of Dragons you can call on. Just like you pray to Angels, Archangels, and Ascended Masters, you can call on different dragons. It is a human belief that separates everyone and everything. The dragons are all ready to work with you on all that you require when it is required. Do the exercises as you deem necessary on your "path of wholeness."

You are very dedicated to a spiritual connection with the elemental realm, as they are also with you. It is amazing, this deep yearning you possess for inner wisdom and knowledge to be awakened. This shall be, and then it will be a "teaching of self" you will offer humanity.

Day 49

Violet, today is a special day, and I am eager for the energy to consume me entirely. I am at peace, and I feel blessed in all that I am led to do. I truly have an alternative belief. Why?

Life is a blessing this day, as you open to the depths of inner wisdom. This "belief of self" is key to all you strive to be. There is no ego at all, as your path in many ways is "full of serving." To give openly and not expect anything in return is of Spirit.

You have nurtured and nourished your soul's growth and expansion by the beliefs in your heart.

The soul is of the heart. It is this "bridge of self" many never cross. It is a choice to cross or not. Many stay in the "body of self" as if the fear, guilt, and shame are a token for who they are here to be.

Opening the heart to love and "crossing the bridge" into that which is truth, through words, insights, and connection to Spirit is of the soul. "Balance of self" is "crossing the bridge" into the unknown to grow and expand as a spiritual being.

Eventually, wholeness is accomplished by becoming "one of self," which is also "one of all." Wholeness is the blessing that one receives. This is not an alternative. This is truth and love that creates and manifests blessing in your life to be shared with all.

Day 50

Good morning, Violet; this dragon book is powerful. I really do not know where to start.

The "journey of self-discovery" is the beginning. This is where you started and continue moving forward. There is an inner knowing you own. Follow your heart, it is the "voice of your soul." Support surrounds you, and all you have to do is ask. Reach out in mind to the "unseen essence of life," and magic will claim your day.

Life is to be lived as a human. However, life is the "spiritual aspect of self" that craves wholeness. It is the "action of self," which manifest change. It has been your path for a long time, it seems to you, but really, it has been a blink of the eye. The essence of possibilities is in the trust you possess that there is more.

Never stop seeking the "inner wisdom of your soul" that needs to be nourished and fed to be whole again. It is to be! There is a path that completes the journey of a life experience, and daily, there needs to be choices of love, joy, happiness, and belief in the unseen world. It is a belief that opens the door to all that your soul desires to return to. Continue as you have been doing daily with your "truth of self."

Day 51

Good morning, Violet; sadness, sorrow, and transition is coming! How do I handle this?

Today, you ask me about sadness, sorrow, and a transition that is coming. Your bond to others on their journey has been a witness of love for all. There is a human belief of sadness and sorrow when a transition begins and succeeds.

This is a joyous time for the one to finally transition home back to Spirit. Fear is a human belief remember and never a "belief of Spirit." The human gets attached to the life lived, but why is the question. The answer is simple, the fear of the unknown.

Regrets play a role in humanity's choices; even their actions in the past haunt them daily as they journey forward. Remember, you are of Spirit, and life is eternal. To incorporate the celebration of a life lived and the love shared during the reflection on a life lets the transition go peacefully. The soul knows when the body cannot endure any more of this life experience.

Pay attention to all that will transpire and witness the fear of the unknown and the attachment that drives the living to fight the will of a loved one. It is this simplicity of believing they have the power to choose and control another; that is the sadness and sorrow they manifest. Choose love!

Day 52

Good morning, Violet; miracles are happening around my life in a sudden and calm manner. Is it all my prayers being answered?

Miracles and prayer, you ask about? There is an awareness of insights in the slightest change in your experience. It is clarity and insight that is granted for the connections you have acquired with Spirit. Praying is necessary to a changed "mind of self." It allows light within to shine out. It is a blessing to be open to the path of the depths of the power within self.

Positive beliefs, words, and actions nourish the soul's ability to inspire you as a human. It is this "joining of Spirit" and human that becomes a new self, a whole self, as a new human. It is this that will eventually be shared to open the world that a new humanity is needed to save all Gaia suffers, so we shall not suffer. It is this moment that is needed now to create all that can be of "light and love" again.

The "miracles of existence" stems from the "magic of self" that lies within and unfolds one's connection is secure. Life is meant to be a calm "journey of existence." *"Free will"* has been destructive for humanity. You can say that humanity has to choose another way of being today to survive.

Day 53

Good morning, Violet; an interesting thought popped into my mind this morning. I am alive again! A sort of renewed me! "I lost myself in the depths of a wounded heart." What does this mean, Violet?

You are questioning the changes and feelings of being new today as if you were lost? It has been a "journey of discovery of self" for you to learn the lessons to be of service. You have been of service to many for different lifetimes. This experience, it was the "lessons of selfless love," an unconditional love for another that has deep karmic wounds. It is a healing for you to survive this relationship whole.

It is a bond derived from "fear of self" that another clings to, while you cling to love as the basis of your existence. One would imagine the power of love could heal anyone. Still, the roar of the ego is loud, constant, and fixed on control. To go into the depths of another's wound is to lose all of self and to come out eventually renewed. It is this journey you agreed to.

Love is life, as God is love. Still, fear overrules the journey because of a lack of responsibility for self, for humanity as a whole. *"Free will"* is the choices given to pick and choose daily one's own experiences and how they think, speak, and act. To awaken to this belief that change is possible manifests an "opening to self" that is new unto itself with love.

Day 54

Good morning, Violet; I am excited to have this entire weekend alone. Is there anything I need to focus on at this time intuitively?

You question what to do to focus on at this time intuitively. Your passion is the written word, and to read and write opens the third eye to obtain deep insight. Pay attention to your thoughts and follow them as soon as a path is revealed. Silence is appreciated as well on a daily basis. Try to be silent with less communication to receive insight, clarity, and direction.

There is much change approaching in your life as you move forward on a journey of the "discovery of self." It is this opening that will fulfill your purpose during this life experience. I feel your smile, and the sparkle in your eye is a twinkle of joy for the unseen world to behold. All that you are today shall be magnified. You have to be ready to accept and be fearless on this new path that you have been guided to.

You are blessed by the "Highest Good of Source" to travel in partnership with the "unseen," as you call us. It will not be too long until we will be seen by you. The windows of your soul are swinging wide open to guide and inspire your words that you so love to share.

Day 55

Good morning, Violet; I am amazed by the thoughts of guidance I receive. Really just whispers from my soul that are insightful.

I feel very humbled by all of this! Yet, I am aware I know nothing and await the opening of insight from you! When is this to be?

Divine timing is the question today? Well, it is a process. A learning for you so that a teaching will unfold. There is a belief in life that the unseen world is all fantasy and not to be believed. Tread lightly now for you are entering the magical, mystical realm of all of life.

There is not only humanity to consider, but the essence of all that lives on Gaia. As we are one, there is no end to that, which is not a belief. We are alive as the trees and forest of nature are—the plants, animals, creatures that live on Gaia, as well. Gaia, too, is a living, breathing home for all as a planet.

Imagine children learning of this new life, and respecting all of the life on Gaia, as *"the all that is"* seen and unseen. It is not new to us, but extremely new for humanity to grasp. Fantasy is real.

The unseen elemental realm is real. The Angels, Archangels, and totem animals are real. Although we are unseen, we journey daily with all of humanity. It is to be a teaching you will learn to share.

Day 56

Good morning, Violet; what a great weekend, filled with insight as to the future journey of my life. I find it interesting, nonetheless. I feel adrift this morning. What shall I focus on?

Insight? Adrift? Focus? Life is very interesting for you at this time as you are downloaded with information from the "realms of Spirit." Know that insight is a claim to the "desires of the soul." Change is a claim to the "desires of the heart." It is essential to ground yourself daily so that you stay focused. Balance is also required so that you do not drain and empty the mind.

Meditation is a tremendous tool that many choose to fear. I find it silly that humans fear themselves. It is the silence, act of consistency, and connection to Spirit that are benefits from meditation. What is there to fear?

Your processes are constant, and there needs to also be time to be human. You are a human being, remember. When "wholeness of self" settles within, you will be able to step above the 3rd Dimensional level of humanity and enjoy the 5th Dimensional and above as much as you desire.

Still, you are to heal and help those on the 3rd Dimensional level of existence at this time. In doing so, humanity will learn from a "wholeness of light" that fear is not necessary or needed beyond the world of 3rd Dimensional. Be fearless! Teach it!

Day 57

Good morning, Violet; there is a deeper knowing that is coming forward. What is required from me now?

A deeper knowing into the "essence of all that is" has opened a "doorway of sight" to better understand the process. There are always steps to walk forward with one at a time, as you are aware. It matters not the length of the journey but the acceptance to change, growth, and "expansion of self." It is a slow lift of the veil that separates human from Spirit. It becomes a remembrance of the "times of Spirit." As all of life begins in the "world of Spirit as Spirit," while the soul awaits the human's connection.

There is the choice of *"free will"* always to decide who and how the human wants to be. It is the desires of the human that either connects to the soul or not. The knowing stems from the "light of the soul" for you now. Your path is bright and beaming wide as you use your gifts with the "power of truth" in your words. It matters not the avenue you choose to express yourself. It is the explanations shared that allow another to think and then choose for themselves. These are the seeds you are planting, which the human needs to water for "growth of self."

Day 58

Good morning, Violet; can I be opening to the Spirit World in thought, word, and action?

You question about opening to the Spirit world this day. It is a path of acceptance to know and teach. It is in the teaching that stems from fearless sharing that fuels your being. You are Spirit first, then "human to be of service!"

The Soul is aware of the lessons learned, as well as those to come. The "Soul is the light of self." "Soul to Soul" that communicates daily with the "core of self" that is pure love. Pure love is an acceptance of one's truth and a wholeness that the veil is simply a thin veil. Yet, many are clueless as to their power to peak into the veil or even lift it.

The connection to the "Spirit of self" allows the thought, word, and action to open, to let Spirit work through you now. It is an agreement made at one time for the human to eventually open and expand to complete wholeness. It is this time you are allowing Spirit to have a voice.

Much "transformation of self" has been achieved by all that you do. It is not Spirit that opened the way, but you, the human who searched for a better way to be and to live. The better way is through wholeness. Human/Spirit at the "core of self" becomes oneness for all of humanity as a light.

Day 59

Good morning, Violet; I am aware of my body and wonder why I am feeling a soreness in my throat. Why do I feel off?

It is a reason you seek to know for how you feel today? The energies of your body are releasing that part of life that can no longer serve you. It is a cleansing of the past. When I say past, it is not just yesterday but many lifetimes of silence, lies, and "fear of speech." This is for your benefit as the higher parts of your physical body prepare for Source energy. This is a reflection of all you desire to "be of service." This is an exit of sorts, an opening to Source to enter.

There is much reflection to release above the "heart of self." The part that is human below the heart is grounded and secure to hold, like a container the new energies that will be coming in. This is a true path of "journey to Source" to heal humanity.

As you rest, reflect and release, know you are safe and protected by the unseen during these adjustments that are a necessary cleansing for the body to now experience. For now is the opening of your truth, passion, and purpose.

Day 60

Good morning, Violet; OMG, I have injured my fingers, toes, and all on my left side. A fever, sore, and I am in pain. Why? Why? Why?

Injuries to yourself, you are asking about this day? It is the thoughts of your human brain, which are very scattered at this time of year that are manifesting injury to your body. You are deeply connected to a life that will be changing. Your soul is aware, and it is preparing you for the outcome of change.

To experience growth in life, there has to be a change in life, thought, word, and action. You are aware of what appears in life through the power of thoughts, especially.

It is more than being positive that has created your life. When things appear to happen, it is the outward attachment to an outcome. Do not think of an outcome or what will be. This is not a real world you are in, so it matters not the outcome manifested by another. *"Free will"* guarantees each gets to choose the end of life, and many are even clueless that they have this power.

That is why this time of year is sad for many. However, their sadness stems from life, liking a past outcome. Being unattached is the path to acceptance and joy.

Day 61

Good morning, Violet; what is going on with me? I feel ill! What Dragon beside you can I work with now?

You are questioning your circumstances and another Dragon to work with? The "release of self" as you have been, has begun. All that no longer serves you physically is being cleansed. Rest. Relax. Renew. Your journey is changing as quickly as you can handle it. There is much teaching during the sleep time that is deeply being implanted for the new you to be birthed.

What Dragon do you feel in connection with? Start wherever you feel most comfortable and continue on. You are given an opportunity to "be of service" because you desired to. It is all that you desire that will now be possible. Rest. Relax. Renew this day so all can be downloaded. If you are open to receive, then you will be gifted all you can handle.

It is a process. It is an opening that you need to receive to do the job you came here to do as a Spiritual Teacher. Stay in the essence of your truth, offering unconditional love to all. Many will benefit from all that you share and need time, as well as for the process of change to enlighten them.

Day 62

Good morning, Violet; I took your advice to Rest. Release. Renew. I chose to do so these few days trying to grasp my karma in this body of mine that is in pain. Can you please help me with further advice, Violet?

Rest. Release. Renew. You ask about your karma this day? You dwell on a belief of unconditional love as a first instinct in life. Others do not. The power you possess stems from your beliefs that many do not possess. You are a human being that deals daily with other human beings. This is a challenge at times, and you fall prey to absorbing others 'words as truth. Truth does no harm.

It is not to be a part of your life experience to become prey for others to feast on. Stay true to your beliefs. Stay true to who you are. It matters not how another chooses to be as long as you stay true to what is the "purity of self" that fuels your soul. What that comes down to, is unconditional love that you possess to share with all.

You wonder why it is yours this beam of unconditional love to be shared? Well, you are a "way-shower" and people, many people need to be clearly shown the way of the benefits when one chooses love first.

Day 63

Good morning, Violet; I have trusted your insight on matters of relationships, and I thank you. How do I open myself to more of Source, insight, and the unseen world?

Many questions have stirred you this day? Do not become attached to objects. It does not serve your soul's purpose. Connection to the "unseen source of life" is a process that is opening. If too quickly, it can be difficult for you to comprehend. The future is unfolding, day by day, to get you teaching all that fuels your soul and human aspect.

The "vehicle of self" is releasing all that is no longer required at this time. In doing so, there will be new downloads as you are already aware of. Slowly and securely, all will be known, for you are to help humanity, but first, you have to learn how to do so in this lifetime. Teaching is the path you have always chosen in many lifetimes. That is why you collect books, as you do.

It is in reverence and respect to the written word that is powerful. As a being of light, your words are now infused with the energy of light and love for all that read them. A sort of energy healing, you gift them now.

MYWOLF

Mywolf stretched and jumped over the rocks to get to the waterfall. He liked traveling to it to check in on Kali from a distance.

Humans were unaware that where they walked a part of their energy remained to offer healing when there is no fear. All Kali had to do was think of her waterfall and love would be felt there.

The power of thought was extreme in all situations!

His life had changed drastically within these last few months since Kali moved forward with Violet.

At times it felt that she was flying forward and so eager to be of service. He was proud of her! He missed their moments together though.

Mywolf imagined the past and the years that he had served Kali from a distance and here he was again observing her from a distance.

The circle of life is for all Spirit and Human.

Chapter Twenty
December 2018

Day 64

Good morning, Violet; is there anything I need to do to prepare myself when it comes to what I will be teaching in the future?

This day you ask about preparing yourself for the future? Your journey is a teaching of love that has no rules, boundaries, or demands. Love for you is the "joy of life." To teach this, you must continue to set an example of loving unconditionally with no attachment to an outcome. It is up to others to choose for themselves as *"free will"* is part of God's plan.

Prepare yourself to teach and show the way but do not force an outcome on another. Everyone shall eventually choose love, and when they do, miracles will be received. As a "teacher of love," that is your main function, to allow humanity to decide for themselves.

Just as you received thoughts to change, everyone does as well. A clear mind is needed. Reading, writing, and prayer and meditation are keys to making "doors of love" open.

There is not a time limit; it will arrive for all, eventually. Life is preparation to "know the self of the soul." Many need to open to the belief of their soul to nurture and nourish themselves. Do as you do that is preparation enough.

Day 65

Good morning, Violet; I can see clearly now! Thank you! I know there is a reason for everything in life. I am open to being of service to others! What now?

It is that which you want to know which will transpire now in your life? Know what you feel in your heart is the "truth of self." Being upset or hurt by another's action is a human quality of the ego. There is no control when it comes to another. All you are responsible for in life is how you react to situations. There is no defending of self when you have always acted with love. Your open heart can easily be hurt and fill with sorrow but is it yours? No, it is not! Stay true to that which is your passion. The release has begun now as you renew yourself to being in communication with "Source Energy."

Many do not know or experience life as you do, and you can only show them the way. It is up to them to choose how they want to live. *"Free will"* is always their first choice. The ego knows this and fills their heads with blame of another when each manifests their lives daily by thought, word, and action. They refuse to accept the power that they have a choice. You see this in many. Their confusion and belief in separation is not yours. Be true to your beliefs!

Day 66

Good morning, Violet; I am starting to feel better, and I am eager to know the plan of service I am to manifest.

Your question this day is how to be of service? Well, you are always of service; every thought, word, and deed are a choice on your path of either love or fear. As a light being, love is a natural choice, but the ego roars out of fear of the unknown. This creates havoc in life for many.

The magic of life is that as a "being of light," your choices have a mystical quality when love is your first choice daily. It is a ripple that goes out to the world as a "wave of light" through the simple acts of prayer, meditation, and sharing love for humanity in all forms.

The "truth of life" is we are all here to determine how powerful we are as humans. Dogs show unconditional love and offer joy to humans. Yet, humans fear to show love to one another. "Being of service" is the acts, thoughts, and spoken that are filled with love for another.

Self is not involved the instant love is beamed outwards for another in any form of acceptance, awareness, or adaptability. Where there is no judgment, one is "being of service."

Day 67

Good morning, Violet; I started adding your channeling to my book, A Key to the Unseen World. I am receiving downloads of supplements I can stop taking. Is this all correct?

Kali, I admire your diligence and insight. Know all you receive is correct for you now. There will come a time to edit "A Key to the Unseen World," and in doing so, the information given will guide humanity to choose another way. The "cleansing of Gaia" and many light-workers has a purpose. It is time for "Source Energy" to fill Gaia and humanity through the gifted ones like yourself.

There is a window of time that is in process, as far as humans are concerned. However, the "reality of Spirit" has no time. Spirit goes with the flow; no judgment, blame, criticism, fear, or anger. Spirit is Light and the way to share Light is through the action of a love that is unconditional. Pure love is Light Love.

As humanity develops an understanding of self, they will choose "love of self." Humanity needs clarity and insight into the unseen world of Light and Love that is waiting for all to claim as Spiritual Beings. There is always a choice and *"free will."* There is no wrong way or right way, for there are no mistakes as Spirit.

Day 68

Good morning, Violet; I have missed you! I am sorry to be a bit distracted, but I have a feeling when you are with me, thank you. Help me, please?

This day, you are asking for help to stay focused? Life has this path of craziness during this time of year. It can be overwhelming, but as you know, I am at all times by your side. You do well to stick to a constant time, whether daily or not, to communicate with me and others. Consistency on your part is "Connection to Source energy." Set a time and stick to it as you have done prior to the "cleansing of self."

The energy at this magical time of year is powerful for humans to withstand. Being grounded helps as well. Your rituals are specific for years, and it is the simplest of acts that you benefit from. This is a teaching in itself to be constant in your beliefs. The thoughts, words, and actions are a vehicle for insight into Source Energy.

Sometimes, a break is necessary, but you must return to the path of your passion and purpose. Many humans are scattered and all over the place, which lessens their ability to change and expand. Consistency, focus, and passion open one to the ability of Source Energy as a download.

Day 69

Good morning, Violet; I am at a point of expansion, it seems to me. What can you guide me to know on this?

How can I guide you through your point of expansion, you ask? "Expansion of self" is the joining of "soul to Spirit" to the unseen. The cleansing you received has stirred up the juices of connection as well. There is now an opening that will fill your mind and heart with clarity. It is the guidance you adhere to that will benefit many. The process is an awakening that unfolds in steps that are available for all, Kali.

It is the clean diet, prayer, meditation, and the inner "wisdom of self" that speeds the journey into a full-blown experience. The path is one you have chosen to walk and is the essence of the "discovery of self."

It is amazing that many refused to change their ways to develop their path and discovery. This is a teaching for you to share. Belief is key to opening to the unseen world. Belief in the journey comes with a plan. The steps are for the human to travel forward, and in doing so, expansion is evident.

Day 70

Good morning, Violet; What do you want to share with me this morning?

Kali, I shall share with you the following this morning… There is a process to the journey of channeling from the unseen. There need be no doubt that I am with you as well as others. Being open to receive from the unseen is the journey to the "way of communication." It is the journey of this "discovery of self" and the past that is now opening to show you the way.

Changes are many on the path of life experiences. Know there is joy in our communications for me as well.

It is the "essence of self" that stirs the soul to know by being nourished by the foods it needs for change, growth, and expansion. There is a stirring within that is surfacing on this undertaking, and I am amazed at the clarity you receive by going in silence.

I see it is not easy with all the challenges many in your life have agreed to experience but never believe there is no hope for change. There is always a moment that can switch on the light within that there is much more to life than pain and misery. Yes, there is a plan and karma to know and release, but anything is possible for those who desire to heal themselves through their own actions.

Day 71

Good morning, Violet; I had an interesting day, as you know. I feel misplaced when not at home. Why?

Today, we will discuss your feeling misplaced at this time. It is an inner feeling of disconnection from all that you love. There is no reason in your heart to travel away from all you love. It has become a" ritual of the day" to do that which is unique to you on your journey. This traveling has never been a desire of yours in any way, so it throws you off course.

The energy is not to your essence. You seem to lack comprehension of the whole affair. The desire for purpose is needed. And, there is no purpose for you to know the answers to all you seek. You can say, "No," and that will be it if you desire.

Your support as a "light being of love" is excellent and goes beyond what is expected. If you cannot handle anything and do not benefit from what another needs to express your feelings with love, I, your Dragon Spirit Guide will help you to open to the trees that you have a connection to. Breathe in their essence and speak to them when possible.

Day 72

Good morning, Violet; I seem to have figured out a connection of traveling to places for another that is not relevant for me! What do you think?

Your wisdom for change is self-evident... You are on target once again. There is an "inner essence of self" that needs less than another. Your comfort and beliefs are enough for you. "Connection to Spirit," writing, reading, praying, meditating, and "being of service" fuels your soul. You are nurtured by these actions and fill with wisdom and knowledge daily, as well. It is a "design of freedom" for this plan to be "true for self," daily.

When you travel to be adaptable for another, you stop most of your nourishment and get thrown off track. It can be a cleansing to step away for some time because you shall return. Still, it changes and stops your momentum. Daily attunement is needed even while in another environment. It is your way to help another, but you can never change another.

It returns to how you want to live your life. It is an energy change as well but wherever you go, know you are a light for others, and you are planting seeds. Look at travel as a disruption in life that is not forever.

Day 73

Good morning, Violet; what is next for me?

Our journey together is the "essence of self" that is open to the world that you refer to as unseen, which is delighted with your desire to "be of service." As we are all here for the same purpose, it is a blessing for Gaia to behold.

We hear your thoughts, concerns, and wishes. As I am your main Spirit guide, work and insight are needed for guidance to do so. It is your responsibility to organize and do all that needs to be done for our book. I will do the rest.

You have been open to these suggestions, and it is the challenges in your life that take you here and there. Focus and consistency are required. Humans have this belief in time that is needed. In the Spirit world, there is no time; there just is. To be is to act in accordance with your passion and purpose. It is your responsibility to write and publish the channeling and communications for humanity to open to a world of your beliefs that will benefit many.

Meditate as often as possible. Go outside as well. The "silence of life" will fill you with deep wonder as a child, which can be a teaching to share. The "joy of wonder" is in life!

Day 74

Good morning, Violet; there is a great teaching I am receiving on the truth of unconditional love. Can you guide me further on this awakening?

This day you are acquiring about the great teaching you are receiving on the truth of unconditional love. You ask for guidance on this awakening? The "truth of self-discovery is love." Love for Self. Love for All. Love for Gaia. Love for Life. At times the lessons in life are not adhered to because the personality gets stirred up to knowing it "knows!" It is the wise choice to accept in life that there truly is a reason for all situations, especially the drama and challenges that arise.

Forgiveness, Acceptance, and Release to an attachment is a glowing beginning that a lesson is being learned. As a "being of light," it is love that is a deep teaching for others to learn. Gather around you all that you have learned by the "simplicity of belief" you possess. It is with certainty that you live your life, Kali. Many do not.

It is a deep awareness that love encompasses daily choices. The complaints of another bounce off of you because of the wisdom from many lifetimes that is part of who you are. It is your "essence of self" that beams out a current of light that is filled with love.

Many have a very different view of love. Love is an act of goodwill for another, a blessing for self and another, joy, happiness, and kindness fuel the "love of self." It is the gas that moves you forward into action, as the gas that fuels your car. This is true love, and you have awakened to it!

Day 75

Good morning, Violet; what information do you have for me on our channeling at this time?

Interest in the information that I have for you on our channeling at this time is your desire? The beauty of your mind is abundant, with an opening to the Spirit world. It is the channeling that, when consistent, will guide your journey. To believe is as important as your daily rituals.

I see within the essence of your "truth of self," the goodness that is to be shared. Your gift of writing heals many, as well as allows a seed to be planted. It has always been a plan for humans to open to the Spirit world eventually.

The purpose of all Religions on Earth is to believe in the unseen. Humanity has taken it to another level by the teachings offered but then leaving it in a church, temple, or mosque.

To believe is to open to the energy of all that is available, alive, and possible in life. Mother Gaia plays a tremendous part in healing you and humanity. The essence of earth, breath, water, and sun are the elements of the elemental beings and the path of daily life. This is a teaching to adhere to. Humanity needs to spend more time outside. To soak in the elements and in doing so, a healing is always possible for the "whole of life." It is this oneness that has to be acknowledged in a belief of, I heal equals you heal!

Day 76

Good morning, Violet; I am having a blast with you! I feel you protect me and take me deeper into the realm of belief that is unseen. Is this true?

Truth is what you seek this day; as to where I take you into the realm of the unseen. The achievements you are making are led by your connections. It is a desire to "be of service" that has opened the "portal for the unseen world" to exist for you now. It is my pleasure to offer you deep insight to share when it comes to belief in all that is not of human form. To believe is to expand, release, and renew oneself on this "journey of service" for humanity.

It is a vision you acknowledge and find a challenge at times with. The "avenue of responsibilities" are all part of your teachings! We, the unseen, surround you and learn from you, Kali, as well. Humanity, as a whole, make very difficult choices for themselves. Your entire existence has been processing the difficulty of those who are not kind or nice. It makes you sad.

Let it be known that you are a "being of self," which is a light of hope for many. They cannot put it into words, but they know you are the "true essence of love and light." Confusion for them stems from their own choices of control. No one is in control, and that is a lesson to learn for many. A plan exists!

Day 77

Good morning, Violet; Can I be going insane in my life of challenges that are not mine?

Challenges in life you desire to know about? Few believe in the manifestations in life are their own doing. There is a mindset that others are always doing something to them. Thus, they become a victim of belief and fall into a path of discomfort around others. Many cannot comprehend that they have no right to control another. In doing so, there is judgment, criticism, and fault that someone is not doing as they need them to do and be. Silly as it seems, why is this?

Fear and jealousy are a dark journey to choose but know there is always a lesson to learn. To know as you do the ability to see the whole picture; past, present, and future is freedom from the choices that others manifest as challenges in their life. These are not yours, and you choose wisely to not take on what is not of your doing.

The mind is interesting in someone who is jealous as their thoughts fill them with the belief that they need to defend themselves. It would be to their advantage if they questioned why they needed to do so. What really is being done to them? How have they participated in manifesting this challenge and chaos in life?

Day 78

Good morning, Violet; I am grateful for you in my life. What is planned for the future?

What is planned for the new year is your question this day? An "opening of self" to the unseen world will change your life as you know it. The process for you is to teach humanity that there is a bigger life and world than what daily living is. The attachment to rules is no longer possible in the future. It is time to allow life to develop from an open heart and mind.

The "soul is of love" and knows the passions that need to be expressed. Joy, happiness, and kindness are the path of change. Many fear to change, but this can no longer be possible. There is a current underneath the surface of all that is required to be ignited now.

A "connection to self" comes first so that love is a choice daily. To let all that has come to be released for remembrance of one's passion and purpose can be birthed. It is a "renewal of life" lived with joy and love filled with wonder. "Connection to self" is a discovery of *"the all that is"* fueled by the "Laws of the Universe," not the "Laws of Mankind." *"The all that is"* surrounds life on earth, and the future teachings you will offer will help with the expansion of humanity, Kali.

Day 79

Good morning, Violet; I am open and ready to hear your thoughts on celebrations humans choose?

Curious to know my thoughts on the celebration's humans choose? Happiness mixed with joy equals love expressed. Humanity loves to acquire material substance and spend lots of money in the form of gifts. Children are filled with wonder at the idea of all that requires a celebration because of the beliefs of magic and a jolly old man. Many refused to be open to those they claim to love. Many betray and do harm to others as well.

The true gifts during the holiday time on earth are ignored. Peace, Truth, and Forgiveness are "gifts of the Soul" that need to be expressed. The "magic of Gaia" is during this month, and all contracts can be released when abuse, addiction, and abandonment are part of a family. Null and void as they say.

No harm to another is a clear statement. Words and actions that are harmful do create pain and fear to manifest. Karma comes from this "essence of belief" in harm. To heal one's karma, a choice of love in life is essential in thought, word, and action. The "wonder of magic and mystery" is abundant in the month of December!

Day 80

Violet, I embrace you when you allow me to know you are at my side. What message do you have for me to share today?

The energy around you is expanding, and many will be drawn to the "light of your heart" as it opens. There is a process to share this type of information, and it is the truth of your belief that allows believability. Humans are in desperate need to change what no longer serves them.

The tools of your life will benefit many as simplicity. Those who need action will adhere to these teachings. Many will need a plan to follow to entice them forward for change. Your knowledge will enlighten those who seek to know as they seek a release. The ones who desire to be nurtured will fly to you on "wings of love" and drink up your nourishments.

The future will be vast in Gaia as a complete cleansing, release, and remembering for renewal. It is time to birth the new essence and choice on a daily basis. The simple act is to "choose love as a being of light." First, it has to be remembered that all are "beings of light." It is this connection to each light within the self that beams out love.

Day 81

Violet, what can I benefit from that I can teach others as well?

It is the "essence of truth" that is a teaching in itself. "Truth of Self" is the discovery that all are required to examine. To know who and what is the reason, purpose and passion are required, as well. There is an energy in life that is sacred to the core of each soul. In a "discovery of self," one meets this energy as their "essence of self, their soul." The soul, as an eternal part of all existence, waits to be awakened by the human personality. When awakened, the soul is nourished by the "whispers of self-discovery." It is the whispers that enable purpose and develop passion.

Those who choose not to know their truth are addicted to a part of humanity that is false, a sort of brainwashing. Beliefs that are handed down and part of life that has been created by the ego of man. That which is truth is love. It is the connection to one's soul that stems from the universe and *"the all that is."* "Love is Soul Connection. Fear is Human Connection." Love is the truth of God as one's Spirit. What is not of love is a human belief in fear and all that stems from the demons in the chakras?

Day 82

Violet, I wonder about this journey and the path I am to stick to now?

Wondering about your journey and the path you are to stick to this morning? Wondering is good when a journey changes, and a "portal to the unseen opens." It is a new path that has opened for you through your desire to teach and "be of service." It stems from your passion as a mystic and seer from many lifetimes.

To know there is a reason for everything in life is a blessing that many do not comprehend. It is why there is fear, guilt, shame, grief, lies, and illusion that many attach themselves to. The diseases of the body stem from their attachment to these beliefs. When these demons are released, the heart opens to love. If love opens all doors in life, one must discover why they refuse to choose love.

It is your path and journey now to teach the release of demons by understanding love is all there is in life. It is not easy for any to grasp, but this is a "gift of empowerment" that is yours to share through the written word. "Being of service" is the "open-heart of self" that is full of love for all. It is "truth of self" that all are Divine, and it is time to realize their Divinity and choose love.

Day 83

Violet, what can you tell me as we come to the end of this year 2018?

Yes, you are curious as to the end of 2018 this morning? Many are awakening to the "truth of self." Look around at all the teachings that are now available. Many have opened their hearts with love for the less fortunate. It is an end to a time of separation that is no longer necessary for humanity to cling to. Many are being cleansed while they sleep to open to another way of being. Many are also refusing help to change.

Opening to Spirit, Truth of Self, and Unity is the beginning. Life is swiftly changing on Gaia, and the elementals, dragons, crystal skulls are those who believe in the unseen world and are extremely busy. As the "vibration of Gaia" raises, humans will also raise theirs. Of course, this is part of the *"free will"* process, and all are allowed to "choose for self."

There are no mistakes in life. Remember, all set their plan prior to arriving. Many choose not to remember and fall into addictions, negative, abusive beliefs, and in doing so, harm to self and others. No lesson gets learned on that path. That is the gift offered by reincarnation for humans. To be born again. To choose another way, eventually.

Day 84

Violet, I am blessed to have met you as we partner in life. What advice do you have for humanity now?

The question you ask today is about advice for humanity? The time is now open for all to start fresh on their journey. Goals and intentions are not the force that is required. "Love of self" enforces humanity to "open their heart" and "embrace a deeper sight."

It is the path of many to expand and grow toward being filled with love. Many fight the simplicity of their own goodness. Fear grips them and fills their mind and locks their heart closed. To "open the heart," one has to realize they are a "being of light" and the key to unlocking fear is love.

The ego roars and fills the mind with needing to control to be powerful. Love is the extreme of power, and miracles are manifested. Anger, abuse, addiction is manifested with the fear generated by the ego. To choose another way is possible for all.

Yet, here we are today with many fearful and locked up in their own misery. *"Free will"* is a gift that is abused by the fearful. Control and a belief in knowing what another must do is simply choosing fear. To live and let live is powerful to choose. There is always a "choice of self" with love!

MYWOLF

Mywolf gathered around him all of Kali's Totem Animal Spirit Guides as the year was coming to a close. They had all spent many years sharing her life experiences and had moved on to other children in need of their magical, mystical, mystery of joy that they offered. Especially at this time, there was a need for dragons and unicorn energy for the children now.

Mywolf ached for time with Kali but a deal was a deal. Violet needed her undivided attention. No one wanted to overload or overwhelm her with the unseen world.

Chapter Twenty-One
January/A New Year

Day 85

Violet, I felt the essence of you in my meditation this morning. Do you have a message for me?

Today's inquiry is if I have a message for you? There is a peaceful energy at this time on Gaia. It is a new day, month, and year for all of mankind. There is quiet contemplation and promise for a wonderful tomorrow. Today is a deep path of reflection, regret, and release for many.

Some will just lie to themselves and say, it is just another day! However, it is a new day in many aspects as one travel's forward with a "belief of self" to make changes. Diet, exercise, and dreams are the focus.

The season called holiday has ended, and in reflection, for many, too much was spent, or not enough was received. Humans are very predictable unless they desire to make a drastic change. Many will! Many will not! Some will try! Some will fail!

Consistency and desire are essential to grow and live one's "truth of self." All are looking for their truth in some way or form in the journey of life at one time or another. If they are not happy with their choices, change is evident, but fear holds them back. Everyone in life is meant to be happy, Kali.

Day 86

Violet, being of service through the written word is a gift I enjoy and love. Are you really inspiring my book, as I believe?

The love of your life is the written word, and you question where I fit in this day? The "discovery of self" for many is by going within. There are many avenues to do so. The "magic of books" is the lessons and teachings one receives. It is a journey that has served you well.

Soon, your book will be ready, and as a Dragon Spirit Guide opening to you, I am to be included as well with the mystery and magical world of the totem animals. To be aware of the guidance received is to be open to the unseen world that surrounds all.

The teachings of books like this is a wonderment to be expressed as well. Belief is individual, and if one is ready to experience change in their life, your book will guide them to believe another way. It is to be!

I am honored as well to be part of this collaboration with you. When there is a deep "connection of self, love and light" beam out to the universe. It is magic at the moment one changes and decides to believe in the vast world that is alive and present to help all of humanity. Love is essential to opening many, many doors in life.

Day 87

Violet, how can I be of service to the fearful humans that surround me?

You want to be of service to the fearful humans that surround you? It is fear this day that many choose as a "protection of self." Fear of love. Fear of happiness.

Fear! Fear! Fear is the first choice! Some choose fear instinctively as a cellular memory. Duality is a process of belief in fear. Those who gather around addiction, abuse, and anger are more than fearful. They are here to release karma created generationally.

It is *"free will"* that is gifted to all to choose daily who they are and how they treat others. Forgiveness must be chosen sooner or later to open to "life of self," which then allows the fearful to love another. The process can take lifetimes. Darkness can only be released by light. All are light that seeks love to blossom into a choice of "Spirituality of Self."

Balance is a path Human/Spirit equals wholeness when duality is no more. There is much to teach. There are many teachers to learn from as well. However, one must be awakened to knowing change is possible, but they must

130

want to change to see the light they carry within. With an awakening to "self-light" comes "self-love."

Day 88

Violet, I am interested in knowing about my soul's abilities now?

Soul work is your question this day? The abilities of your soul are beyond earth and the existence of your life. The soul is eternal love and focuses on bringing light into your life. To be a "being of light" with a "mission of awakening" is due to *all* that the soul has experienced. Lifetime after a lifetime, your soul's eternal journey has guided the "essence of human expectation."

To awaken to know your soul is the first door of many that love opens. To experience this change is to know that there is more to your existence in life. The human as a vehicle for the soul is pure light, at first, born as a baby, to develop *"free will"* to experience the lessons chosen by "self of soul."

Challenges and chaos have all been agreed on but forgotten. To Be Love, one must Choose Love.

As a spiritual being manifesting this human experience, you choose love, joy, happiness, and kindness. Taking these now as teachings out into the world is your soul's ability to inspire, guide, and empower you. It is part of the plan that your "Soul as Spirit" has chosen. You are Love! However, first, you are Light, Kali!

Day 89

Violet, what can you tell me about "Oneness?"

"Oneness" it is this day that you inquire to know about? "Oneness" is the "essence of life" in all forms on Gaia and the unseen world as well. "All are One!" It is a process of belief, though, that many refuse to discover. Separation is chosen because it fuels humanity's ego-self.

Belief in negative thought allows separation and not "Oneness." It has been a given that duality is the foundation in life, a choice that there is either or in life—a complete belief in a system that has developed in humans that there is good and bad.

In a belief in "Oneness," there is none of this. For all are "light beings" complete in their "Oneness" of love. Where there is love, there is no duality of belief. It simply is a fact. Love is all there is!

Many are experiencing this light that now is abundant on Gaia for animals, the earth, and when there is a tremendous loss of human life. The next step is to know that, "Oneness" is for all; human, animal, plant, Gaia, and even when there is no tragic loss of life. There is a lesson in all that happens on Gaia to discover that there is a reason for all. The plan is for humanity to awaken to a belief in "Complete Oneness."

Day 90

Violet, what is now expected of me as I do the channeling?

Expectation is what you what to know today, Kali? Awareness always to your thoughts, words, and actions. Stop when you feel off your truth. Be open to receiving. It is a path you travel now that is expanding, and the books you read will be insightful. There is truth within that comes from all that you openly offer to others.

You are a "being of light" first, then a human, but balance is needed to offer the love of self as a teaching to others. Set the example with an "open-heart" for much is being downloaded during the sleeping times. Meditation will help in this deeper expansion. You are a "lover of ritual" and prayer, which serves you well.

Bring all of this out in Mother Gaia, and you will serve mankind well. It is a deeper belief in "Oneness" that you are experiencing now. Dedication to *"the all that is"* can be of service for you as you go deeper into the "laws of the universe" that differ tremendously from the "laws of man." The Spirit of many is sleeping. All that you do for self is slowly awakening many, due to the "light of Oneness" within your essence. You are light! You are Love!

Day 91

Violet, why is it that I am so happy?

You want to know why you are so happy? "Fulfillment of self" creates the happiness you question today. "Connection to Spirit" is a path of joy as well. Why should you not be happy? Are you not doing all you desire?

132

The "journey of self" is a deep discovery for a process of change to now emerge. For a change, action, a plan, desire, wisdom, and knowledge are required. With an open belief for life, everyone discovers their "self-mastery" to be acknowledged.

Much focus has gone into all that you experience daily, and the end result is happiness. There is a gift when one lives their passion and knows their purpose. This gift is a life filled with light connection to this light, which comes from within. It is a freedom to have no fear and to benefit from the ability to share as a teacher.

As a distant healer, you heal through your thought (prayer), word (writing), and action (energy). This is tremendous focus on your part. Remember, consistency is part of awareness and discernment to live the life of your dreams. In doing so, it is happiness that is experienced because "light of self" is loving the daily activities as a passion-filled experience. It is a journey of "discovery of self" that is most feared. It all waits within, and one needs to "connect to this light within," eventually.

Day 92

Violet, when will I know it is time for my book to be ready to be published?

Hmmm, books and publishing, you question? I am the Dragon Spirit Guide, who protects you at this time and is part of your story to share? The day will come when the "inner light of self" will awaken to the release of your story. It is this belief in the unseen world that will "awaken the wonder" of many as children. The timing will be soon, and I am proud to be included.

There is a tremendous advantage to telling a story of the Spirit world and all that is but is unseen. Many will get a moment to reflect on their own delight in certain types of animals throughout life. "Remembering of self" is the journey to release. In doing so, renewal and a rebirth of truth will manifest. There has always been the journey, but the path will lead all home.

"Change of belief" is the essence of all "truth of self" to awaken. If all have a gift, passion, and purpose, they will discover it eventually through all that is now available worldwide. Books and teachings, combined with the vast classroom of the internet, are the future.

Day 93

Violet, Do you have a message for me this day?

You have a question this day? Yes, I have the following message for you! The changes within that are surfacing have been manifested by all you do daily. There is the journey, but what one walks on their path of this journey can be magical. Love stems from the light within. As you have connected to yours, the magic is arriving.

Many humans stay on the merry-go-round of daily pain. It seems they believe in some way it is deserved. The victims in life have chosen to be victims. It is the path of all to find their journey to *"connect to the light within."*

Fear, guilt, and shame from yesterday's choices stop them from moving forward. Much can be taught that each human is a part of the "Oneness." Once it is chosen as a "belief of self," connection will follow, and the "light of self" will be a path of love to be shared with everyone.

The main tools that you acquired to remember to use daily have been prayer, keeping a journal, and being out in Mother Gaia. These are the "magic of life." Adding on meditation and "ritual of sacredness" with a positive thought process has brought you to this page.

Day 94

Violet, it seems impossible at times to help a loved one in a dangerous situation. Can you advise me on this?

Danger in life is a deep question you are concerned with? It is a journey that begins in all relationships until the pain and fears of one partner need to be numbed. Demons of the mind affect many that are negative, abusive, and angry at themselves. There is also a plan that has been desired. The minute or better the second abuse of harm on another arrives, the plan is null and void.

Everyone is a "being of light." There are no exceptions. A mistake is never possible. All are here to learn the lesson of love that joins all in the realm of "Oneness." Darkness of the ego fears "Oneness," fears "Love and Light," especially.

It is the human being that strives for understanding that is fueled by the ego as well. The plan is to grow, expand self, open to Spirit, and remember it is a plan. Release of everything and everyone allows remembrance and a "renewal of self."

If you feel pain and harm from another, then they need to be released from your life, for you are not being served by them. It always comes down to the human discovering how they want to live this life now.

Day 95

Violet, I believe you have a message to share with me this day?

The message I have for you today is as follows! The fire within that ignites you to be you is the ability to "trust in the process." Belief is the platform that is most believable for you. "Belief of Self" allows your passion to create. "Belief of Life" develops the purpose of your soul journey. To enjoy daily the ritual of creation by bringing the elements of Gaia along grounds you. There is an inner knowing you possess that enables insight and clarity for you to share.

Communication through the written word is your deepest and greatest gift. You are clueless as to all you heal by your words. This is a platform you desired, and it is now active because of you.

There is focus and consistency with a ritual to "honor all of life." Many do not do as you do daily. Your dedication is powerful!

Stay true to you these next few months with a balance in all daily choices to achieve further direction and insight. Clarity is yours to hold and bestow on others through words. Humans need to be awakened that life is not as it seems to be. There are reasons for everything. Yes, there is darkness that many choose; however, the "power for change" is to "choose love," which stems from the Light.

Day 96

Violet, I feel different? Can you explain to me why there is a change in me again?

Change and being different is what you seek an answer to? It is the opening of a life to inspire, teach, and fill with passion that creates a deep change. Preparation and all that you choose as the "basis of self" creates a difference within that stirs the soul. Silence in meditation opens self to the unseen and unknown.

To be aware is a gift you possess daily in all you strive for. The energy of belief surrounds you in its fullness now. You are never alone! It is a path filled with tremendous light.

The "Oneness of Self" is the difference and change that has arrived. There is insight in all that you desire to read. When you write, it is of healing for another who reads. The "journey of self" as a "being of light," love and oneness manifests miracles now. As you expand and teach, more will be experienced by those you offer yourself to.

To be love is to know one is love. "Love of self" is what stems from unity and a belief that all are of light and desire connection through love. The "Oneness of Self" is the unity of love joined with pure insight of belief that truly, there is more to a life experience as a human than one can imagine.

Day 97

Violet, I am ready to learn all I can to astral travel at night. Can you help me?

Astral travel is the question you ask about this day? During the night, you travel to school to learn the wisdom within. It is to be an opening for all that is to be. It is a form of travel that many light-workers experience. To remember is the opening of one's portal to *"the all that is!"*

Many do not believe as you do. It will be when you are ready. There is much that is happening in the realms that are not to be known at this time. The future holds the mystery, but the magic is to be exposed. Astral travel is to be in the future, and you will delight in it.

Humanity is struggling daily by choice. Many are filled with duality in all areas of life. The personality of their ego-self is empty of belief as you desire.

Still, all are "beings of light" experiencing life here as a human in matter form. All are not ready to know as you desire to know.

The journey is to release what does not serve. To remember one's truth. In doing so, a "renewal of self" allows belief to change and to know anything is possible, especially astral traveling as you desire. It is to be!

Day 98

Violet, is there a message for me this day?

This day you are asking if I have a message? We, as a team, have developed a process that you have committed yourself to. It is this belief in me as your Dragon Spirit Guide that opens the portal for this channeling. It is a deep belief of remembrance of a time long ago that is now surfacing for you. Look around at all that you are attracted to in books, music, and movies. It is truth that all is not exactly as it seems in life.

The Soul knows as the "Spirit World" is real, and the time is now to share the insight of our communication. There is only a belief in "Oneness" that needs to be realized to open the portal of the unseen world.

Many are clueless because of the existence of their lives has been formed and handed down generationally. Many choose to cling to what they know is fact but that which is not their truth. The "ache of self" within scares them that there is another way to be.

"Free Will" is not doing the same thing over and over again and being unhappy. *"Free Will"* is to choose another way to be happy. *"Free Will"* is to offer Love to self, to love another, on this journey of being human. To "know self" is the beginning of true manifestation and deep healing. Bless the challenges and move forward to a "journey of truth" through change.

Day 99

Violet, I know when you are with me now. Can you offer any guidance?

It is an enjoyable time now that you know when I am with you. The guidance for today follows, as it is a fun ride, we are filled with deep adventure.

As any choice comes from self, you must stay consistent in all that you desire to manifest on your divine path. The journey will unfold totally in divine timing. Sometimes the ride stops for introspection, release, and remembrance. Knowing the ride will begin again is the "opening of self" to remain focused always.

There is no end, only the "journey of living" all that you planned prior to your birth. The "clarity of self" is belief. Once your "portal of mind" opened and let me in, the ride started. There is an excellent "understanding of self" that is developing now. No fear means there is only love. Where there is love, there is light.

It is an amazing choice to teach the "world of Spirit." Opening to such a sharing is a blessing for many. As you heal, all heal through this belief. Trouble yourself not, for all, is on its way to be shared through your beliefs. Knowing in sacredness, as the path of this ride, you are blessed by all elementals, angels, totem animals, and spirit guides to be all you strive for.

Day 100

Violet, this is our 100th-day channeling. What is your message for me?

It has been 100 days of getting to know one another, and my message today is: Begin the journey of your teachings now as a channel. It is to be shared through the written word. Gather around all that serves your soul's passion. Your toolbox is expanding with belief, insight, and clarity of the unseen world. You never alter and are very consistent, teach the power of this!

Arise to the heights of your truth in all that you have accomplished. There are many challenges humans face, but going within for answers empowered your journey. Teach that which comes from "connecting to the self of soul" now. All fear has been erased by the belief that only love is possible. Being aware of your thoughts has gained you an inner path to your purpose and passion.

Writing is a tool that has empowered many as you share. To share is to "be of service." To know "life is sacred" and that all are lights waiting to be ignited is a teaching as well. Show the way by belief, thought, meditation, and asking for help, as has been your journey. To be consistent, focused, and passionate has been embraced by you daily, and look where you are today because of your beliefs.

Day 101

Violet, what can you tell me about multi-dimensional humans?

Curious about being a "multi-dimensional human" this day? It is so, for where one looks at life on earth as a school with many lessons to learn, there is "power of self." Fear that gravitates that life ends and one needs to be in control is filled with fear and anger in most situations. The journey of a loving non-reactive human is one who does not fear, anger, judge, or criticize due to their beliefs. There are many who travel through life with a wounded heart and mind, so to speak. Their fears eat at them, and they walk the path of no power of self.

Many adhere to life outside of themselves for the answers. The simple act of going within is a "multi-dimensional human" that knows they need to heal first. In doing so, those they call family will also heal in the future as well as the past. A multi-dimensional human has many facets to discover.

The emotions of fear, pain, and anger need to be studied and released if you are ill or unhappy. Know who you are and how you want to live your life experience is the path toward a "multi-dimensional existence." "Belief of self" by going within is the beginning of a life of love, joy, and happiness.

Day 102

Violet, your voice is clear and different in tone as you share information. Is this the teachings for humanity I am to state?

It is about the information I share with you and the teachings for humanity's growth that you ponder this day, Kali? It is to be as I share, for there is a reason for all that is written. The process is unfolding for you to begin. Already you are opening to a deeper belief that all is never as it seems.

Prepare yourself to live your truth and to walk your divine path. It is yours to claim. Many will heal from all that you can offer. Many have begun already! Once they begin to believe, they too will ask and receive. They must now awaken to their truth, passion, and purpose.

Everyone has a gift to discover. First, to realize and accept, they are a "being of light" to share "love of self" with all. The journey is the awakening to a belief that is theirs, not one that comes from another or society as a whole.

All that has been written and spoken of love is the "simplicity of life" that ignites peace for all on Gaia. There is no fear ever when one knows their "truth of self." It is my teachings that you shall teach through the word.

Day 103

Violet, I feel that you have a message for me since yesterday?

This day you notice I have a message for you since yesterday. It is a great tribute to me that you are aware. I fill with love and joy for our connection. It seems you struggle with the demands of change when it comes to traveling away from your daily existence. I was supporting you as best as I could to visually know I was at your side. Recall, I always have your back.

Your beliefs are powerful, forceful, and literally expanding. At this time, much is asked of you as well as being downloaded by all that you are learning to share. Sometimes change benefits the soul to relax and simply enjoy the ride as a human.

"Boundaries of self" to do all that you require for self is to be your priority. It is the tools of ritual that benefit your journey. Don't go off your course for another. I shall support your choices and guide as best as I can to calm the "essence of change" that affects you for these days. Breathe in the air, move to stretch the body, and add a sense of joy that this change is temporary, and all will return to fulfill your purpose.

Day 104

Violet, I appreciate your guidance and support. What do you want to share with me today?

This day you seek a message from me. It is your connection to self, belief, rituals, and open heart and mind that benefits your path. "Source Energy" is a portal above that serves those who desire to be of service for the good of humanity.

To be open to guidance, clarity, and inspiration serves you well. There is a "depth to life" that is not of Source Energy, and when this is known, inner wisdom arrives with the "Spirit of Light." The simplicity of belief is a requirement. All one has to do is release the beliefs of humanity that are not of Spirit.

The "Laws of Life" are Universal in the world of Spirit and never fluctuate. Man's laws are consistently changing per human. Many do not stay focused or do their due diligence in life. It is their demons that rise and twist their minds every which way. This is not the journey to "Source Energy" opening for them.

"Truth of Self" ignites with "Love of Self," allowing a knowing of one's "Light as a Spirit" to shine out to the world. It is a journey for all to seek and discover.

Day 105

Violet, it is an awakening for me to serve you at times. What brings you to my mind?

Your awareness of me fills you this day, so it seems. I appear in a flash when you need strength and protection from the humans in your life. The karma of challenges can be many that appear for another but are not yours. Your "way of self" is grounded and, at times, can feel as if you are stubborn. Kali, this is not so.

Your reason for "journey in life" at this time is to be the one to empower others with your light. The very second you are aware of, all you know to help ignites the sense of me in your mind. You are never alone. You are protected and guided. As you ask, you will receive.

Many do not ask because they choose not to believe. Your "belief of Spirit" is your greatest tool in all that you manifest. The portal is thin in life, and there is comfort in opening to the unseen world as part of your life experience now.

Have fun, laugh, and love with the wonder of your inner child not stubborn but "powerful of a belief" and "way of being." To "know self" is the journey you manifested as part of a Spirit functioning as a human to be a healer of all Gaia and humanity as we partner together.

Day 106

Violet, I feel disturbed, and I do not know why? Can you help me?

This day you question how you are feeling at this moment within. Well, it is a lack of familiar space that troubles you to tighten your grip within. Try to wrap your mind around the belief that nothing is permanent. The "journey of self" expands on change, which offers growth. Relax into yourself that all you can be and do is yours wherever you travel to. Opening to the "Source of Life" is available wherever you are. "Divine timing" is for all and possible only when there is no anger or resentment in life.

"Opening self" to do the work you desire is possible because of you! There is no denying that you are walking your path fully by all you are learning and setting up as a teacher. The "freedom of self" has been ignited by your choices. Look at your situation this day with an "open heart" and balance out your path in all that is being manifested.

There is no doubt of self now. Your inner wisdom has arrived. "Divine timing" supports you. Connection to me has opened your mind to know and see anything is possible. Your writings are of the light and healing. Power is yours to share for all finally.

Day 107

Violet, I have settled into traveling away from home. What is your message today?

My message today is to breathe, stretch, relax, and open to a "life of manifestation" daily. All the rituals that you deem necessary in life are required to stay on course. As a "sacred being" experiencing the sacred in life through ritual, you stay grounded in your truth.

To look and see all that is along the path to guide and inspire is a "beam of light" for the journey. A blessing, healing, or prayer for another is a belief within the soul that is eternal. We are all eternal as we are all part of an existence that has been planned to now awaken.

Gaia is cleansing herself as humans need to do as well. The words of your mind stem from your heart and soul to be read by those who are clueless that change is a true release of yesterday. All that is not of love needs to be released for the expansion of the human who travels a fearful path.

It is now time to open the "portal of eternal laws of the universe" to release the "laws of man" that are harmful. Man's way is no longer a "path of truth" and needs to be released. In doing so, one by one, humanity will open to the "self of truth," which is light and love.

Day 108

Violet, why do I feel displaced?

The rituals of your "existence as a mystic" support you this day and a feeling of displacement is the "energy of change" that surrounds you. In your mind's eye, "Life is sacred," and all you do is sacred. The existence of sacredness rests within the "temple of self."

Displacement for you is being removed from that which, for you, is the sacredness of your day. Simply put, you feel out of your "sacred space." Much is missing from the energy of all that you treasure. It is a feeling of emptiness that is generated by displacement or change in your environment. In all reality, it is energy. The energy does not soothe you as does that which you are accustomed to on a daily basis. A mystic needs silence, ritual, and a feeling of "connection to self."

Bring in your "essence of light" this day, Kali, through the adjustment of your mind that you are the "temple of self" wherever you are. The environment has a different energy that is not of your liking but go within to that which is comforting.

A mystic that is "true to self" exists on very little. That which comforts and fuels you are a simple existence surrounded by all that you love and are passionate about daily. Feeling displaced does not serve your energy field.

Day 109

Violet, I called to you in the evening while I felt I was being attacked by another's projections of fear on me? What is going on?

You question today a new challenge in your life! The wounds of humans are deeply embedded from lifetimes. Fear, anger, hate, control, and jealousy feed their mind. Many are unaware of their inner light because of their beliefs. To be so angry at self is their way of being that they project out toward another. To grasp happiness, they need to change. However, change is filled with fear at any age. A closed heart suffers from a closed mind. Control haunts them daily to do as they do toward others. A belief of failure is evident where there is no control and this angers them.

Those who lash out suffer deeply because of a belief in "separation of self." They have no "unity of belief," only one that is to be in control of all. To believe is no connection to self or the elements. It seems from them that life is a struggle. They live to work, and then they will die. There is no pleasure unless they rule, and all obey. It is a vicious pattern that fills them to lay dormant, and they sleep until they awaken to attack because another is happy and they are not. They have to make a change. Fear fills them up because the familiar is what they crave. What would they change, and how do they change is their "question to self?"

MYWOLF

Mywolf walked slowly over the path of the waterfall feeling deep within the struggles Kali was facing. It was a gift to have such a deep connection with her energy. To know she was on a tremendous learning curve with Violet at this time as her Dragon Spirit guide, pleased him. Mywolf embraced this journey as the path of Kali's destiny to unfold.

Her struggles were based when she was out of her sacred space as her home fueled her with an emptiness to return due to persecution in past lives she experienced. She always desired to be safe in her home.

Chapter Twenty-Two
February 2019

Day 110

Violet, what do you think about last night ritual I performed?

It is an interesting time for you to release all that needs to be let go only because of the teachings you will receive. "Cleansing of self" is an "act of love" for your temple. Be open to this guidance for rituals are the fuel for "self-integration."

It is a unique belief of yours to follow your path with daily "discernment of life." Many humans are clueless about this "power of life" that is possible by releasing the day by the act of water. Energy is all around, and to travel through a "portal of infinity," the temple must be cleansed and anointed. The "release of the day" will allow "remembrance of self" to then be renewed to walk a path through life as a Spirit.

The temple is temporary but picks up debris from darkness and negativity that is part of life's *"free will"* daily. To travel to the night on an astral plane, one must be cleansed of the day, and the room as well has to be free of all disturbances.

The dreams of the night are signs for all to do what needs to be done in life. Many do not believe as you do and negate themselves as well. Humanity as a whole does not connect to the "Spirit of Self" day or night.

Day 111

Violet, I find that it is difficult holding space for another who fears life?

Why is it difficult holding space for another who fears, is your question, Kali? The challenges and chaos of life is "fuel for insight." It allows you to be aware of the battles many struggle daily within. That is why the saying is, "To take nothing another says or does personal."

The journey of all life experiences is to untangle what is not your truth. To discover the "path of wholeness" through your personal emotions and beliefs. Anything is possible for one who opens their heart to experience love. For the one who holds space for another is a challenge of patience and compassion. To open self to another's fears is to know it is not yours but theirs.

Life is a journey of connecting to another's "inner light of self." All are light. All do not choose to ignite their light due to their karma. The challenge is to remember self has a purpose and gift to discover, which stems from loving what you do.

Those who are angry, hateful, or unhappy do not love self or their life choice. Regrets fuel their mind, and wanting to be the best is a plan they cannot achieve where there is darkness. Look at darkness like a black cloud that hovers over a fearful human with a closed heart. Once their heart opens by their choice, the "light of self" fills with love and dissipates the black cloud.

Day 112

Violet, I am grateful for you and have a deep inner knowing now of the ease and grace of life. How is this possible?

Today you ask about the possibilities of your life now with ease and grace. It is the inner "essence of protection" that I provide for you during challenges and the inner struggle of another. It is a "light of love" you offer and are very honest in your daily beliefs of the fears of many. To see their fear so clearly and not judge another is a blessing you offer.

In doing so, it is I who protect you to not blink but to be you. It is a strength you possess since a child to be of service by offering love. Many are clueless about the harm they project on themselves when fear is their choice. It is the fearful that can be draining for others as they are toxic in many ways. Who are

146

in pain are filled with darkness and fearful beliefs! It generates from the depths of their temple that is not honored.

Thoughts, words, and beliefs that are empty of love fuels their ego and degenerates them from the inside. The fear settles as demons of the chakras and fuels the inner organs to break down eventually. Anger and resentment are not ever yours, so you are protected from those who project that outwards.

Day 113

Violet, Thank you for protecting me from a challenge that had no effect, but simple information of another's fear. I feel blessed!

Kali, you are feeling blessed this day! A challenge that can cause a confrontation to separate one from another empowered you to speak your truth. In standing in "power of self," filled with the wisdom of another's fears have led you to be strong.

When I have your back, you can feel the heat of my fire travel up your spine. In doing so, there is no anger, only "truth of self" that you are able to express. There is no need to understand another's choices but to let them use their *"free will,"* as needed. It is never your place to take another's *"free will"* from them.

The adventure you chose to experience in all you do for years now was your desire to share information to help another. That is what a "way-shower" is in truth because you desire no reward. Your greatest teachers have led you to this "path of self-discovery," and you never faltered but moved forward seeking all the wisdom and teachings that have taken you this very moment on your adventure.

Being "open-hearted" has a tremendous advantage compared to a closed heart. To cleanse yourself at the end of each day will benefit you to connect with love and shine your light with those who desire to "change in life."

Day 114

Violet, there is a deep understanding I am experiencing pain because of another's fear. Can you explain this?

This day the pain manifested by fear is what you desire to know about?

The "heart of humanity" is love. Where there is fear, the heart shuts down, and a "portal of grief" sits within as "fear of self." When there is fear, abuse, and blasts of ugliness, one creates an inner pain that flows through the body and disease manifests. Pain is manifested by belief that is not of love. To attack or deny another *free will* is fear. There are many diseases of the body that stem from "choice of self," spoken, acted upon, as well as the "inner thought process."

As a human who no longer believes the human way, your light guides you now. It is a connection of wholeness that has manifested by the rituals of your existence. To be alternative is to not need to punish for "one is free" in all the totality of their existence.

You are experiencing a complete and love-filled existence by the "light of self" that life is not a separation but complete wholeness when love is chosen. Love simply is. There is no other definition. To be open is to have a heart full of love to help another who fears and manifests pain and is clueless of their power and truth. It is a human blocking "Spirit of Self."

Day 115

Violet, what is your message for me today?

Kali, my message for you this day is, be aware as a change is upon your life circumstances. There is no need to not live your truth or feel that you are inadequate. That is no longer your belief. The truth of your being is a deep love that goes beyond unconditional, for you embrace love as who you are. The light you shine out is crystal clear, and many will heal and embrace your teachings. You have done the work, and your focus and endurance are unique to your journey.

The path is golden now because of your beliefs and challenges you embrace with compassion.

Your "freedom" is your belief that comforts you as the only way to live in truth. When you walk your path with your head held high, I walk with you. We are a team now, and we shall survive all change that is required for you to "be of service."

Finish this book, "A Key to the Unseen World," and gather it together as a whole. It is time to do so. The next book waits to be shared as the truth of all you believe in, as well.

There is no other way for you to live, but as you do in all your thoughts, words, and actions. Patience for you is natural, just like breathing.

To be you and manifest all is part of your destiny. I have your back and stand with you daily.

Day 116

Violet, will I know when these channelings are no longer part of our book?

This day you desire information on our channeling and the book. The teachings of the book are profound insight into a life that is unseen but greatly functional in life as a whole. There is a "map of life" for each individual that leads them on a "journey to the key." Walking and existing daily through the "map of choice" can be open to travel, collecting the key needed to open the "doors of connection."

Many pray to their unseen God, Goddess, Saints, Angels, Archangels, and such. The unseen world of Spirit, elementals, dragons, unicorns, crystal skulls and others await recognition to help humanity now. The "elements of life" and the "elementals" are part of the earth, water, fire, and air. All are real but unseen, Kali! The trees, plants, and flowers are full of "elementals" that serve Gaia and humanity.

The key to gathering along the "map of life" is to "awaken to sight" that is open to all of the treasure life has. The fairy tales and science fiction of life are real and part of the basis of life's truth to be realized. I will guide you to know the end when all is covered in the words you write. This is a wake-up call to humanity to awaken to their purpose, passion, and truth of all of life on Gaia.

Day 117

Violet, what is the meaning for this portal, and is it from my highest good?

You question the meaning of a portal that you see and if it is for your highest good today? "Source Energy" of *"the all that is,"* has a gift to offer you for your diligence in accepting all challenges with love. The mind is a portal to the divine. The portal is a place of comfort that keeps the wisdom and knowledge you desire to share. It is a "journey to a realm" you know and long for. The light of your love that you bestow is the opening of such a portal.

To be so adaptable, acceptable, and compassionate has brought you to the next stage of your journey. Access to the portal is clarity, insight, guidance, and truth to be for you to share. The portal is the "realm of mystery" now but shall be the "magical essence of a true existence" as a "Spirit of Service" to humanity as a whole.

Many are aware of your gifts and how you can show up now. The process is always connection and acceptance of the "unseen realm" that is not seen but can be seen eventually. The portal is the first step into the realms and world of the unseen that is real. "Light and love" are always for your highest good as you cleanse and prepare yourself nightly to enter the portal. Stay open. Stay true to self. Prepare by the act of cleansing with water and anointing your temple with Essential Oils, Kali.

Day 118

Violet, what is the reason that I do not always see the portals?

Today, you question why you do not always see the portal? There is an energy of negative belief that is not yours that needs to be eliminated. Where there is darkness, the light is feared. Continue as you do to benefit that which is needed to raise the "vibration of unity" in humans.

It is the thoughts of a negative person that is literally poison to the body. This poison is a darkness that eats away at the body and mind. "All souls are love. All souls are light." It is the back and forth motion of letting fear come and go that does the most harm.

"Portals of light and love" are an experience of joining the ascension of all that is possible for humans who stay true to the essence of their soul's teachings. Unfortunately, the battle within most is a belief of duality; good/bad, happy/sad, ugly/pretty are comparisons of one believing one knows.

There is no knowing whenever there is a "belief of unity." To be of "unity belief," all is one period.

To be open to travel the "portals of ascension," be "true to self" as a "temple for all life" on earth.

"As you heal, we all heal," but each must choose their path proudly within their heart.

Day 119

Violet, Thank you for the guidance I know comes from you. How does channeling play into my experience now?

With thanks for me, you ask the question of how does channeling play in your life experience now? Kali, there is an "essence of your life" that is empty, and channeling has come forward to fill this void that is no longer necessary. Where there is love like yours to offer to others, the receiving is a requirement from *"the all that is."* *Channeling* is a part of that which is your "love of self" in a matter of words. Your temple and sacredness are honored now. Rituals fuel your daily life, and so a ritual of channeling has been given to you. Is it not powerful for you to behold?

I am part of this journey, and there is no need to thank me. The truth is that I thank you for believing in me. There are many who struggle their entire life empty of a belief that they have the "power within" to choose how they personally want to live. Your choice to want and need a reason to share as you termed it, and in doing so, opened yourself to the "inner wisdom of knowing" how to do so. To take the teachers in your life as the lessons you needed to learn to change, expand, and even for the "ascension of self" is your soul's desire to be honored.

Day 120

Violet, Can you tell me what you know about all that is transitioning in my life?

You question what is transitioning in your life at this time? You are on an amazing ride that is changing daily by all you believe. The awareness, focus, and commitment to yourself in the "form of ritual" is serving you well. There is a deep knowing that is developing that will help you in the future months.

No attachment or illusion will benefit your coming adventure. As you know, all is a "journey of inner discovery of self" to share with all. As you learn, you will teach! Dreams do come true when there is consistency, light, and love on a daily basis in all that you desire to do and be.

Those who fear are clueless about their power because they do not know who they are or what they can offer in life to another. It is the "belief of fear" that grips the mind, and they become stuck completely in a "pattern of negativity."

To teach them to love themselves first is incomprehensible to grasp because fear closes the heart. Where there is fear, there is guilt and shame. Regrets play a huge part in the life of the fearful. To release fear, another has to be chosen and adapted into their daily mind to "open their heart." This is love, and it is possible for all to choose.

Day 121

Violet, what can you tell me about all that I experiencing?

Your curiosity, this day, is delightful, Kali! There is expansion, initiation, and higher vibrations being downloaded. That is the reason you feel sleepy and fall back to sleep, actually. Your mind is totally open now to receive.

As you continue your daily/nightly rituals, you are aware of insight and guidance. Life is to be enjoyed. Love comes from the essence of your light fully activated. There is change and transition now to "complete wholeness."

A "type of shield" has been placed as a way to contain all that is needed to guide you in your learnings and deeper wisdom. The knowledge you crave is "truth of self." Your path is widening to include a vastness of sight, travel, and teachings. Being open to the journey is the belief in gathering the path you are to walk in the future.

Many do fear their future because of this attachment to material belongings, people, and especially that they are not being "true to self." They, in reality, refuse to choose another way due to their fear. To open to love is a choice!

Day 122

Violet, what advice do you have for me about my choices now?

Choices and my advice are a curiosity today? Let me see how I can "be of service." There is an "inner guidance" you listen to at all moments of unkind information. It is that which you ponder.

Then your choice is to "choose love." Yours is an "open full heart" with a deep "desire to serve." However, you acknowledge the "truth of life" that it is not your responsibility. In an instant, you receive the thought of *"free will"* and the "lessons in life" all have agreed to experience.

Of course, you can offer to help, advise, and even connect people to others with love for all. Still, you realize that is all you can do. These thoughts are like the fluttering of a butterfly's wings. Quickly you release them, for to benefit your journey is to show, not control or take on another's choices. It is the human journey to desire to know what is best for anyone. No one knows another's plan or path. Many have karma to cleanse. Many have "love of self" to embrace. All have *"free will"* to choose as you do.

Day 123

Violet, can you tell me how I am doing?

This day you are doing a "journey of discovering" what has meaning to you. All of life's experiences have a reason for being. Imagine:

- What makes you laugh or cry?
- What is it that fills you with love?
- How do you react in all situations daily?

There are many moments in a day where you have to "choose an emotion, a feeling, and a way of expressing who you are." The question today is, do you know who you are? The answer will give you an insight into how you are personally doing.

In your case, you are expanding yourself out into the "universe of life." This can be scary, but it is the "human self" that hesitates when it comes to change. The "Spirit of Self" applauds all that you manifest with passion and purpose. It is this inner knowing that waits to be shared.

Many fear the unknown "essence of life" and have no connection to Spirit and fear the quiet self that is passionate to create. I would say this does not describe or define you at this moment.

"Belief in Self" is a true energy to knowing "Spirit of Self." At this very moment on the stage of life, I would say that you are doing very well, Kali!

Day 124

Violet, what can you inspire me with at this time?

Inspiration it is you desire this day from me? Notice the "magic of life" you are drawn to in movies. Magic is "life's mystery." Magic opens the mind to a belief, of all that is life, is not true. Magic plays a part in the unspoken existence of past lifetimes. It has been a truth for those who believe in their "power to manifest." Magic is the "essence of truth, belief, acceptance, and desire."

Life has many moments where magic was unseen, and disbelief harmed the thought process as being impossible. Many believe they are lucky or not because they are unaware of this power. At one time, all were filled with "magic to create," but darkness stepped in, and "separation of belief" changed the "love of magic" as the "essence of life." Magic exists in truth where there is love joined with the "beam of light" that is the "essence of living one's truth."

I am magical, and I create magic within your mind. Why? Because you believe and remember a time long ago from a place far away that was filled with love, belief, and magic for all.

Day 125

Violet, what is your belief on disease of the body and mind?

You question my beliefs on disease of the body and mind this day? It is a process of another planting a seed of judgment, criticism, and abuse into the mind. It is then watered by the human over and over again like a vicious cycle of thought for years—sometimes for lifetimes. All are born "light and love" and come to learn the "lessons of their karma." Those that carry disease of the body refuse to learn of another way of being.

In reality, sometimes, it cripples the body to the point of deep pain. Disease is in the mind, first emotionally connected to the chakras. In doing so, where there is no change, growth, or "expansion of self," then the human suffers. All have the benefit of *"free will"* to choose every day as a new beginning. A place to start and choose another way.

Sometimes, the mind is so dark and tortured; it cannot grasp a "speck of light" in their world. The darkness settles like a cloak covering the body in pain and disease to the "point of transitioning" this life and get to try again.

Everyone gets to try again and again. The "process of life" is to learn to "open the heart" and "embrace love."

Day 126

Violet, can you explain to me how I am doing when it comes to my passion and purpose in life?

To do! To be! To learn! To share! To be you is an "inner passion" for "truth of self." There is a purpose for your existence. There is a purpose for all who live on Gaia this day. To discover the joy in knowing one's purpose is extremely beneficial to the path one travels. The "map of life" has many choices and directions to travel. To choose a "path of self-love" is a knowing to travel one's purpose.

Is not passion uplifting to the mind? Does not the heart skip a beat? Passion is a clue to everyone's purpose. To do! To be! To learn! To share is your "passion of self and purpose in life." Do you now believe the path you have traveled has brought you home to today? You ask me today, "To explain how you are doing?" I ask of you, "How are you feeling?"

The "journey of discovery" has no expiration date; it simply just is. As it is a "knowing of self" that allows change to lead to growth, "expansion of self" and a "beam of light" are to be shared outward toward the path you travel forward in life. The map is a "treasure map" for all existence to embrace and "discover self-love" first. Imagine this map with its assortment of paths one gets to walk through at different stages in life along the journey!

Day 127

Violet, can you speak to me of my inner wisdom!

You desire my thoughts this morning! Kali, the path of your choice has magnified into manifesting your dreams. It has been a "journey of light" that has shone on the map of your existence. As you strive to be better and grow, the path widened into the "journey of truth" for you. The "Temples of Life" chosen enabled the path to comfort your inner child of pain from many existences.

This map is across many lifetimes converging at last to the present. It has been an awakening that can only be described as an "ascension of your light and love for self, as well as humanity." It is a "state of belief" that has inspired you to travel the "depth of self" to strengthen the "human existence." In doing so, all has been released.

Where there is no fear, only love exists. Many are clueless to this fact of belief that there need be no fear ever, once love is chosen. It is the easiest choice and the most difficult for most. The "map of life" is to discover the "depths of self." All that is necessary when it comes to living a "life of Spirit" filled with joy, kindness, "passion and purpose for self to share."

Day 128

Violet, I feel your joy in our collaboration. Is this true?

Joy and our collaboration are your questions this day! It is true! This ability you have achieved to know me and experience our collaboration as a team is very joyful. It is joy that fuels the life of the unseen. Many would not believe this is possible. Wait until they read this book!

This is a "map of a journey" all in life experience, yet they are unaware of the guidance that is possible if they just believe and ask for "insight of self." All maps have a purpose and path filled with the "pinpoints of time" where a thought, experience, or joyful, loving memory felt right at the given moment. The "map of life" is to become awakened to the times with a "sight of seeing" and believing the path is to be enjoyed. The path is wide and, at times, bumpy, but there are moments that fill one with joy.

These are the grand times to remember as one traveling along their path. It is a release of that which is not serving the human and so they "return to their truth" and walk the "path of self" again and again. This is the journey to be for all. It is the moments where there is light, love, peace, joy, happiness, etc., that all need to become aware of. Many get stuck in a negative belief of fear, anger, hate, and envy. These are not the "pinpoints on the map of life." Ignore them! Release them!

Day 129

Violet, what is your take on the darkness path many choose to walk?

This day you are interested in why someone would choose to walk a path full of darkness? A closed heart cannot breathe in the body that is filled with a "darkness of self." Many who walk daily on this path manifest and "feed the ego." The ego is the control of fear, and darkness of thought fuels the flames. It is carried within the thought process of the belief in not ever having enough or being enough. It is a vicious cycle of blame, criticism, and judgment that they have no control in their life. They seek to control others because of this lack within self.

Kali, blame is a tool that flows from them out of fear that another would know their unhappy and fearful existence is by their own choice. That which controls them now is their ego-self! The battle is to stay in the darkness. Separation fuels the "journey of self" because of the truth that they are alone at all times in their mind because they have no control.

The addiction personality cannot turn on the light to see self is a "being of light!" Self is born a "being of love!" Self is nurtured by "acts of love!" There is pain within if love gets into the darkness for a second. It is uncomfortable to grasp. A dark path is their choice because it offers comfort to the "mind of self" and "feeds their ego to exist" without a need for another. There is no trust that another could actually offer them love. The thought is, *"Why would they?"*

Day 130

Violet, what can you tell me about all that will change in my life now?

A question this day, concerning change that you are feeling? Well, change can be for the "highest good of self" when there is passion and purpose. Other times, change can simply be out of fear of the unknown because work is needed for true change for the "highest good of self." Many, out and out, refuse to change their "way of being." Simple steps can help.

One who desires to change can begin with one "aspect of self" as in their thoughts. Thinking only loving, positive thoughts as much as possible is a change for the highest good. Adding in an "action of love" and support for another and not requiring acknowledgment is the beginning of a way of being and change. How one speaks to self or to another can be with kindness and love because they are doing the best they can at all times.

Picking one aspect to "change of self" is a beginning because the pattern follows all when it comes to consistency and focus to desire a change. To live "one's divine path" as a "being of light and love" is to ascend and awaken to the belief that all are one. "Unity for all" is a complete change for the journey that needs to be embraced now. In doing so, the change that follows appears as if the "light of self" shines one's path forward, and there is no going back.

Day 131

Violet, what is going on in my mind, conscious and subconscious, when it comes to my choices at this time?

Today it is about your choices at this time, and whether they be conscious or subconscious, I see? Let us go to a time in your life where abuse, abandonment, and fear ruled. There was an emptiness in the "hollow of self" that was sadness at all times. There was a desire to know why people acted unkindly. Why were they not nice? The questions you asked became a choice to know the answers. It was the inner cry and "whispers of your soul." Your inner child was a being of "light and love" and made a choice to be a better you.

Through the help of your connection to Angels, Ascended Masters, the Blessed Mother Mary, Jesus the Christ, and Totem animals, you survived the chaos and challenges. Why? Because you asked in prayer, writing, and reading of spiritual books for answers.

It is your desire as a "being of light" gifted with *"free will"* to choose for self to now be a "being of service." Many years ago, you asked for that which you could share with the world. You wanted and needed to "be of service," and here you are this day.

It is an adventure of "truth of self" that has risen to be shared as true "freedom with wholeness." This has been your path in life for many lives, and you have been granted your dreams and desires because of the choices you have always chosen.

Where there is Love shared, there is "being of service," as well. Whether this be conscious or subconscious, I would have to say your subconscious fuels your conscious self to be aware at every given moment that you are offered a choice to make daily now.

Day 132

Violet, how are we doing with our channeling and our book at this time?

Kali, you question our channeling and our book this day? It seems we are a great team, Kali! It is a giant acknowledgement from you to share this information. The passion you delight in is delightful. There is an inner joy in all that you put your heart into accomplishing. We, as a team, need one another. Now that the portal is open, it is my "being of service" through you "being of service" that will be shared with all of humanity.

Yes, it is a magical/mystical world filled with fantasy at times. It is this that fulfills the wonder as a child again in life. To be open is the key. To choose love is the door that opens with this key. Many fear what they cannot see, touch, and know, as a "truth of life." That is where the fantasy slips in, but what if fantasy is the "truth of all existence?"

The books and movies of Science Fiction are not fantasy but a look, a peak, into what is. It simply is the truth that the unseen world exists. This is the truth of our channeling and the purpose and passion in our book.

Day 133

Violet, I am excited and nervous at the same time. Why?

You want to know why you are excited and nervous at the same time this day? The path of all you do now is part of your purpose. As there is joy in living one's dream, take small steps to actually enjoy all that is being birthed by you. The fire within, once ignited, blazes the path and opens to all that you can achieve. It stems from desire, passion, purpose, and doing it all with love.

You are expanding from the girl of yesterday's fears to your complete "wholeness of truth." Kali, you are an open vessel for "Source Energy" and the unseen world.

It is an experience at this time in your life that is exciting. To be nervous is the thoughts of your past trying to be heard. They are not true. They are not needed. They do not serve you. Keep them away!

Reach within self for your connection to your Soul and feel the embrace offered just for you. The many Totem Spirit Guides, Mywolf, and Angels applaud your path and celebrate the part they played through your journey.

Is this not all part of the "discovery of self" to believe no one is alone and can receive insight, clarity, and guidance when they "open to the unseen world" and ask for help?

MYWOLF

Mywolf was humbled to have been part of such a plan. He knew humanity needed guidance forever but to open himself to Kali was a tremendous gift. Humans traveled a journey lifetimes after lifetimes not realizing that an unseen world existed for them. Kali was open to receive and now will share these teachings in her story.

Mywolf was aware that it was time for the human race to acknowledge the elemental world that was unseen by the simple reflection on gratitude for the earth kingdom, water kingdom, fire kingdom, and air kingdom.

Mywolf looked at his reflection in the waterfall and knew in his heart all that humans imagined was real but yet they struggled with their own power.

Chapter Twenty-Three
March 2019

Day 134

Violet, how will I know when our story ends?

You question knowing when our story ends? The story never ends. Life is a process of one's truth. One's truth is the "discovery of self." When one opens to the "unity of their wholeness" filled as a "being of light and love," the journey is reborn. It is a magical/mystical reality of connection to the "realm of Spirit." For in the "realm of Spirit" waits the truth of all life, Kali.

It is "discovery of self" as one opens to the "portal of the unseen world" that is a reality to grasp. It is written, one needs to ask to receive because one has the gift of *"free will."* If you never, ever ask for the help, the answers for your inner innate wisdom, you will not ascend or awaken.

The soul is eternal, so the story never ends. The human part as a vehicle/vessel for the soul changes. It is a deep process of getting to awaken to *"the all that is,"* by becoming aware of the desires, dreams, passion, and purpose that will "raise one's vibration for ascension." The belief that one is a "being of light" here to be "love for self and others," enlightens the "path with unity" for all and a strength that," all are One!"

Day 135

Violet, I felt you yesterday, and it was wonderful. Am I right?

You ask questions about that which you know the answer. It is a verification for many to receive. At the moment you believed I was with you, that is your answer. Our journey is filled with moments where I will let you know that I have your back. For this is my purpose and part of our partnership.

To create and manifest for others to believe they need to know as you do. It is not so difficult to become aware and pay attention at all times. What is needed is the desire to do so! Trust that there is more to life! Believe that the more in life is the unseen guidance that waits for all.

The simplicity to begin is to meditate, be in silence, and ask to experience a sign. Then pay attention with an open mind. "Love of self" empowers one to "choose for self," to be witness to who they are as they are.

Life is a game every morning when one awakens to begin again. It always returns to the reactions one chooses in life. All challenges are a means of "awakening to choose love." This is the simple rule in this "game of life."

Day 136

Violet, my question is, what can I now be downloading daily and nightly?

You are aware of the downloads daily and nightly that you are now receiving. This is true! This is necessary to do the work you desire to help humanity. Your awareness level is filled with clarity and insight. The "portals of light" especially are the openings of your "inner wisdom." The words you write. The speech you speak. The mind follows the "love of the heart." The heart listens to the "voice of the soul."

The clarity of understanding is the "essence of the unseen," as the seen for you in mind, benefits mankind. There is no turning back. As you move forward daily, the past is erased. You have taken the lessons learned—accepted guidance from your Totem Spirit Guides, Mywolf, and now me, your Dragon Spirit Guide.

Think about this "discovery of self" that delights your heart with love for all. Imagine not ever realizing that you were never alone? Can you? Of course not! It is inconceivable to you today to have lived in a world that had no magic or mystical belief to support you. Kali, the ride and adventure and opening to the unseen, has brought you to this page.

Day 137

Violet, what is your message for me?

Yes, Kali, I do have a message for you this day, as you inquire. The time is powerful as the Spring Season approaches for all life on Gaia. It is the "rebirth of life" in many areas. To breathe in this air is very powerful as it is a change of season that brings the thought of many to look within as well. To change, one needs an action, as well as a plan. To "nurture self" with the nourishment to fuel the body, mind, and soul is a teaching that is needed. Many are not aware of all that can create wellness daily.

The rituals of focus allow consistency to benefit your daily activities. To want or desire the communication with the "unseen world" delights all your senses. It is a "journey of discovery" toward peace, joy, and happiness when insight becomes a daily experience.

To hear the word of another and know they believe as you do is true "opening to spirit." It is an awareness that," All is well" for many—especially the children of today who have struggled but open their hearts with compassion for one another. Many adults can learn from the children of today because they are open to "be of service" to help humanity "choose love" to choose another way completely. Many of the children today are here specifically to "be of service to enlighten the old thought process" that there is always another way when one chooses love first.

Day 138

Violet, what have you to tell me now?

Kali, you want to know what is needed now from you? To be honest, I must say the way is set as you continue daily with all that you do. The mind, at times, likes to travel in "reflection to the past." This is true for all. However, the past cannot be changed. It can only be a glance into that which has inspired you forward.

It is said that actions speak louder than words. The actions of the past, if not true this day, can now be forgiven and accepted as a step to move through lessons needed to learn. There is only a "forgiveness of self" and those in the past that have been the greatest of teachers for you. Today is the present that is inspiring the future.

It is the truth of awakening to know in life that change is required when one is unhappy, fearful, and basically unwell. All are gifted within to find their "freedom through their passion." A simple question to ask self is: What fills me with passion? Look at your life and the passion for books, which has led you forward your entire life existence. It would seem silly to miss this passion you possess for the written word. When you open to the "truth of passion for self," the universe welcomes you with open arms to show you the way.

Day 139

Violet, I am experiencing a bit of confusion when it comes to life and bitterness expressed among humans! Why do they not choose acceptance for each other?

Confusion, acceptance, and bitter humans are your concern today, Kali? Well, it truly is human behavior to experience whatever they can in life due to *"free will."* It is much more difficult to be bitter toward another. This confusion you are experiencing is due to all that you know is not beneficial in life. To live with love, joy, and true delight, one cannot be bitter. "Acceptance" is a keyword toward one awakening. It is simple for you to accept because of your beliefs.

The work that humans who are most bitter could benefit from is meditation. Those who refuse to go within can never know their truth. To "live with truth" is to open to "inner guidance." Meditation is a good place to begin. Embracing the beauty of all of life as essential is another.

The steps that need to be taken are not of a difficult nature in any way. However, one has to begin with accepting that a change is required. In doing so, they can renew themselves to "remember self" by releasing what is not their truth anymore. There needs to be a belief in trust that there is a "process to life."

Day 140

Violet, what a chaotic day was yesterday. Why is there chaos in life?

Why is there chaos in life, you ask? Look at life that is portrayed daily on the news. It is fear-based. Many who gravitate to all they read in the news and hear live in worry. It is fear from the moment their day begins. It settles into the energy of those who have no idea that they have a choice on what they put into their minds.

Money issues create chaos for some. Anger, hate, and, betrayal, are a form of chaos that eats the mind. Throw in addictions caused by low self-esteem, unworthiness mixed into the pot, and ugly chaos is consistent. What chaos is can only be described as a deep mistrust and belief that one is a "light being born" to experience love as well as be loving.

A war exists within the self, daily especially, if one is not of the right mind due to addictions. Fear is the power that holds them secure in who they believe they are. If there is chaos, fear, anger, hate, and "betrayal to the self," only they can make a change. Many do! Many do not!

Day 141

Violet, can you help me understand how I am doing?

You ask about self? Kali, you are on purpose now reaching out to "be of service!" The past is slowly drifting away from self as a thought. You have embraced the lessons, forgiven what was abuse, abandonment, and challenging, to know. You have now become "witness to self." This self is light, sharing love, and many absorb all that you offer. It no longer serves you to visit the past. Let it vanish!

There is a release that allows all to remember one's truth. The "magic of life" is the mystery that there is much more to experience. In reality, life becomes a "renewal of self" that one embraces and shares as the path of all that is possible when the demons are refused entry into the mind.

There is no other way to be now, but for you to travel your path. There is only the desire for you to be living your "truth of self." Joining with the world that is unseen will now be seen by you.

Open further your belief by opening your mind and heart for all to witness that," change is a gift" one gives to self. It is a tremendous "expansion of self" that is now moving you forward. Just be true to your beliefs and be a light for all.

Day 142

Violet, how powerful our connection is! How is it possible that there is so much clarity for me now?

The "journey of self-discovery" is a process of following the "map of existence." There is a beginning when one awakens to realize the "eternal gift of life" is for all. It is a powerful connection that takes work and due diligence. Belief is unique to the "awakened one." It is the moment of comprehension that allows clarity to arrive.

The map of your journey has been the path of unlocking all the doors with a "key of self-love." Has it not been such a "magical map full of light and love" that filled you with desire? The passion and purpose of life can be part of this discovery when one begins to live with daily ease and grace. This is a "truth of self" that one embraces to share.

The map is that which allows one to travel the bumps and twisted paths of life not as a challenge but as a lesson. Many get stuck in the mud and cannot discover their next step. There is no clarity if one does not open to "self-love." It is this "game of love," all must desire. To "love self" opens the "heart to love." With love, clarity exists.

Day 143

Violet, help me please with my purpose after our book is done.

Kali, you seek help from me this day. Stay on your path. That is your purpose. There is a journey you have embraced that has brought you to this day. It was not easy! All change has a time of adjustment and a "learning to receive."

Do as you have always been capable of experiencing in the past. The energies you are settling into do not serve you. Being open to knowing offers clarity. Awareness comes from within. Stop, breathe, meditate to stay focused on all you strive to achieve. There is support from the "unseen world" whenever you ask for help. You must ask!

You must open to inspiration. Although it is learning you are experiencing, believe in yourself. Just go for it, and do it, of course, with love! Remember, there are no mistakes. This is the time to enjoy all you have desired. This is the beginning, which allows you to be fearless. To "be of service" is to "open your heart" completely, as all are "souls of light," just like you, and are learning lessons. Be patient with yourself.

Day 144

How can I share my truth and not be on "Push" toward another Violet?

Kali, you are a gentle "spirit of light and love." As you have a fire within to share your "truth of self," I would do as you choose in the written word. This channeling is a book of truth comprised by the "mind of Spirit."

It is the "inner life of thought" that has brought you to believe in the "power of the unseen world." To dream of being supported by the Angels and Saints of yesterday! To open to the joy in collecting totem animals of pigs, monkeys, and symbols that inspired the path. The magic of life takes place and roots itself in the "wonder of childhood."

To believe is to live with Love as a foundation and a choice that Love is the way! Love is the way!

- Love has the golden power to unlock all the dark doors and challenges.
- Love eliminates fear, doubt, and despair.
- Love is a choice that exists at all times in all experiences.
- A simple thought, word, or action, comprised with Love, has allowed the "journey of truth" to be acknowledged.

You are never on "Push," no one ever is when they share their "truth of self," embraced with the "magical golden power of Love!"

Day 145

Violet, change is stirring within, and I anticipate a deep opening for me with you? What is this to be?

Your insight and awareness allow you to be open to change without fear. It is a deep quest for you to seek all that you desire to "be of service." This opening you anticipate in knowing about is of the change that will be in your life. It is awaiting the unknown tomorrow that is in transition today that is stirring.

As a "whole human of self," Kali, your insight is a daily blessing for you. However, you do drift from dimension to dimension, as you are aware. This is due to the teachings you are learning and all the work you desire to adhere to.

Ritual, prayer, meditation, reading, writing, incense, essential oils, candles, and the elements of Gaia support your path as a "world of beauty." This beauty allows you to appreciate the human "journey of life" that most struggle with daily.

However, those who struggle balance the ones who do not. It is this that is steady in life for many. You are comfortable in your relationships because of the love you offer all. Change is the greatest experiment on everyone's journey to accept.

Day 146

Violet, as you know me and my thoughts. What is your message for me today?

The challenges in your life are the moments to "choose love." As a "being of light" here to "be of service" by offering these teachings, you are always protected. The "magic of your life" is the plan you created. It is the "mystical awakening of self" to know "truth of self." Today is the day to embrace all that is offered to you with love.

You seem to wonder at times how your life will unfold. I tell you it will be all that you desire it to be and more. The "map of your travels" has had a winding path that has opened a "belief of self." The discovery of your path to open the journey to today, you manifested. Yes, there was fear, abuse, abandonment, tears, and despair yesterday. Today, there is none. Why?

Kali, you looked at life with the wonder and simplicity of a child. Love is in all children and waits to be ignited at any age. The "comfort of love" is to "embrace self" with the "magic of self-love," which mystically allows love for all to develop as the deep "discovery of self." You have done the work!

Day 147

Violet, there is so much to comprehend on this journey of discovery? How is it possible to teach this to humanity?

So, teaching it is, you inquire about? All are teachers! It comes down to the subject you choose to teach. The "opening of self" to the "unseen world of Spirit" is a vast "teaching of belief." The magical aspect of your existence has brought you to believing you have guides, angels, elementals, and a Dragon Spirit Guide, me, supporting you. Why do you believe this?

The understanding for the students that will arrive to learn these teachings is the "mystical aspect of life." The path to this opening is belief, is it not? Children all believe in Peter Pan, Tinker Bell, Super Heroes, and invisible friends until a certain age. Why do they stop believing in the "magic of life?" The fairy tales in books and movies are true.

The teaching of the "unseen world" is for those with belief, imagination, wonder, and a desire to "discover their truth." To be open, it is time to remove the masks they wear as protection.

There is no need for such masks when one lives their truth by offering forgiveness for all the past pains experienced. Opening the "heart to love" allows a release to experience that there is more to love, more to life!

Day 148

Violet, how are we doing?

There is a change that comes upon you when not in your own "space of light and love." It is time you realize you carry this "space of light and love" wherever you are. There is a different energy, and you feel a "loss of familiarity," but this is the "discovery of self" that shows you the way. Some things work, and some do not.

Open your mind as you always do, Kali, to simply follow the "guidance of Spirit" wherever you go. Stay true to your rituals and cleanse and anoint as well. Yours is a temple, and you are responsible for it wherever it is. It has been a unique experience for me to witness the moment you connect with me. That is fulfilling for this partnership. As I am a guide for you, when you reach out to me, it is a form of asking. When you ask, you receive.

I can only help when you believe I can because of *"free will"* to choose for self. Many choose not to know; therefore, they never ask. All that now inspires you is to be manifested by you. Do as you desire in all circumstances through your choice of thought, word, and actions. I am here for you at all times, just ask!

Day 149

Violet, why do I have trouble sleeping?

The "energy of change" stirs your human self to assimilate into the surroundings. There is much that is different in this atmosphere that affects you daily. It seems to be the "energy of travel" that stirs you off track. As much as you try to follow the "ways of self" with your rituals, it is off-balance. Another drains your mind with constant negative projections. You are protected by many, but it still is heard.

Sleep is the time of "travel to other realms." With doing so, and daily disturbances, your sleep is disturbed as well. The stirring within is for silence, reflection, and intense connection to "Source Energy" now.

Many support you and the choices you are making in the manifesting of your desires of being creative. This takes "energy of self." This pattern will not last forever, but it will not exhaust you either.

Do all you can do to sleep well. Use your tools of calmness, incense, and insight to all that you desire to cleanse, purify, and anoint your temple before retiring for the night. Relax into knowing that, "All is well." You are safe! Protected and supported in all you "choose with love."

Day 150

Violet, I am receiving lots of downloads and information! Can you explain this to me?

The "expansion of self" has allowed your vibration to increase at this time, Kali. There is an openness that has been gifted to your "belief of life." It is all that you embrace now as your journey that are the "teachings of tomorrow." The wisdom that is being downloaded is as old as time. It is this that has triggered you to seek to know, to be, to share.

"All is well" when you open to the "benefits of a connection to the unseen world." To hear is one thing. To listen and act is "change of self" that embraces another "way of being." "Love of self" has encouraged your discovery of the "power of life" open to *the all that is* possibly connected to "Source Energy."

The downloads are a "truth of self" that has always been yours to remember. You are on a "journey of releasing" that which no longer is required.

The remembering comes in now as the truth of your body, mind, and soul. This is now a "renewal of self" to live as a "being of Spirit" sharing, light, and love for humanity to learn as you have done wonderfully.

Day 151

Violet, your power and guidance are deeply appreciated at this time! How are we doing now?

Kali, the path of your journey is widening to encapsulate all your dreams. We, all who support you, are aware of your "sacred gifts." That which will allow "significance in life" we bring to you. It is not just I, Violet, your Dragon Spirit Guide alone.

Your team includes all your Totem Animal Spirit guides, as well, and led by the Master, Mywolf. Although they are the yesterday that was desired to inspire you, they are today still of service to you, if you require them. It seems your focus now on "me" has pushed them away but know, once a Totem Animal Spirit guide is of service, they can always be called on. This is information that is not known by many.

To know is to be aware of "life choices" that are current. Once one moves forward, the choices change because "change is life." This is the "truth of the discovery of self." Reflect on the insight, clarity, and guidance received by the "unseen world."

You are never alone, even if you feel lonely. It is the ego that chooses to guide you to stray from your path by offering a negative belief. Shake it off; clear, clear, clear, all that is not sacred to your beliefs today.

Day 152

Violet, why is the insight and clarity now so clear?

Your awareness is on target daily now. The portals of the "mind of God" has been opened. The path of your "discovery of self" is abundant with light to brighten the journey you are now willingly opening to. It is a dream of yours to do so for a very long time. To travel through this life experience now with ease and grace is greatly appreciated by you.

It is a manifestation of yours to be open to the "unseen world," which offers inspiration and clarity. Remember, you have always been connected to the unseen world since a child, Kali. It was a vivid imagination that let you welcome into life your totem animal Spirit guides one by one.

It was not clear why you were drawn to them yesterday. It simply was joyous to allow the energy of each to embrace you at the time. Today, life is now clear when you smile or laugh at the sight of an animal or symbol of one because they have been part of your "life journey."

It is laughter filled with love for all animals that fill you with "wonder like a child," although you are now an adult. The "clarity of life" is to fill with "wonder as a child" would, at any age.

Day 153

Violet, with all this insight and clarity that I receive, I ask if I am following the right path at this time?

I ask:

- Are you happy?
- Are you filled with passion and purpose for hours?
- Does the time fly by as you perform your rituals, writings, and prayers?
- Is meditation insightful?

I believe, Kali, that you have answered "Yes," to all of these questions. In doing so, your path at this time is exactly right for you.

There is no need to question yourself when all of the above fills you with "ease and grace." The joy of the day sprinkled with happiness is all supported by the "unseen world." As you believe and follow all that opens your heart for love of life, the path you travel is filled with "golden light."

To know one's purpose is that which one is passionate about is always the right path to follow. Hold your head up high as you journey forward filled with insight, belief, clarity, and a deep connection to Violet, your Dragon Spirit Guide, and all from the "unseen realm." Consistency and focus are the strong gifts that move you forward and open the way for more to come your way now.

Day 154

Violet, crazy day yesterday! What do I need to know about the changes I am now experiencing?

Kali, there will always be "change in life" because it is a complete process to do so. Your beliefs are manifesting on purpose the changes you need to "be of service for others." The dedication, focus, and consistency allow the next step to be seen, and it is your awareness that spins you to change again. The "unseen world" is aware as well and waits for all to be manifested.

This amazing journey of your "discovery of self" has been in the works for lifetimes. Never is it a sudden "awakening of expansion of self" that is possible. There is no going back when the key opens the door to the "unseen world."

The map is followed although at times difficult to maneuver but once acceptance that there is more to life as in the "unseen world," it is the key which opens the majestic, magical, mystical realm of Spirit, Angels, Elementals, totem animals, Unicorns, Crystal Skulls and Dragons like myself, to be part of life as a human!

This is why there is a "map and a key" to open the "realm of the unseen world of life" for all to discover. Truly it is a "discovery of self" once the key is discovered to the "unseen world."

Day 155

Violet, I had a great day yesterday. I thank you today for having my back. I feel that I am not getting something? What do I need to know to move forward with ease and grace?

The "truth of belief" in knowing the moment a thought is received is the portal to the "opening of trust." Simply believe in the "process of trust" that you do know, as you hear or think something to be. The journey of "true discovery of the self is trust."

The "unseen world" is aware of the challenges in life for many. Yet, many do not comprehend their part in manifesting these challenges. All of humanity is powerful, Kali. All have the insight and clarity to choose daily how they want to live their lives. When the "opening of trust" is a reality, life simply moves forward with ease and grace.

"Acceptance" allows no challenge and no confrontation. Where the heart is open flows love. Where the heart is closed, love is waiting. Everyone has the joy of choosing for themselves. It is this "process of life" that one knows but chooses to not trust what they know as truth that stops the process to move forward daily on a path of "discovery of self." Meditation, prayer, and journaling help to listen to what the self knows and to trust the information.

Day 156

Violet, where am I being led to now?

The journey of your path is widening to now include the "essence of complete truth of self." It is to be a teaching for humanity to do and learn these steps. To teach and write what one experiences as a change in their life is proof.

- Humans need proof, Kali.
- Humans cannot function unless there is a known reason for certainty.
- Humans desire significance, and many believe they are not capable of change.

However, change is always embraced in fear. Where you are now as a human signifies no fear. The "journey of your path" had fear which you released! How you did so is the teaching now.

Return to the self of your "inner guidance." Your, "IAM Presence" and share the "power of connection." There will always be the ones who fear, no matter how much proof is presented. It is evident that you are aware of this and simply embrace them in your love.

This, humans cannot comprehend simply because they are victims to their "ego of control" and their belief that they are right and another is wrong. Kali, you are powerful in acceptance and are now open to all that will be a future teaching when one believes in the encompassing of the "unseen world."

Day 157

Violet, change is powerful but does it come with clarity, insight, and guidance?

Listening quietly in meditation will empower your path of change, Kali. In reflection to yesterday, simply embrace how you have been empowered today. There are no errors on the "path of discovery of self." There is definite guidance at times.

Along the journey, the moments of clarity and insight are embraced as a simple thought. What is change, Kali, but the "truth of self," adapting to "awakening to the path of one's discovery?" With such a discovery, the "sacred gifts" are acknowledged and inspired to be shared.

- Change is adapting to everyone's purpose with passion daily.
- Change is saying, "Yes" to learn all one can to "be of service" to another.
- Change is a love of life for all.
- Change is the deep inner knowing that one can know their purpose and strive to be of service to all.
- Clarity, insight, and guidance are within self, as one is empowered daily in all they choose to do with love.
- It is love that fuels change, truth, and discovery of self within the "embrace of the unseen world" that applauds you now.
- Change is that which empowers your insight into "knowing self."

Day 158

Violet, what can you tell me about respecting the rights of humanity?

The basis of humanity's rights is their choice to "choose for self" as the gift of *"free will"* is for all. To respect another's choices without judgment or criticism is difficult for many. Kali, you are an example of offering respect for those you love to "choose for the self." This is not so for many. It is an awareness that has benefited you, especially during this lifetime. It comes down to the basis of thought to do "no harm" to another.

Respect of another is given in all challenges that another has manifested. It is allowing the path of another's journey to unfold as they desire it to. All have certain rights that are theirs to project out to the world. Most do this daily through their thoughts, words, and actions they choose.

Where there is fear, beam love. Where there is illness, offer to heal. Respect all who have manifested their daily existence with love and support. Many want a certain outcome to take place, but that stems from the ego of control. Respect does not stem from the "ego of self" but the "god of self."

MYWOLF

Mywolf closed his eyes as if to dream of Kali and how she never asked any questions. She was always so accepting and capable of going with the flow in life. Mywolf was very proud of the journey that he helped Kali to manifest with all the Totem Animal Spirit Guides he gifted her in life!

Chapter Twenty-Four
April 2019

Day 159

Violet, what is your input on the last few days?

Kali, there are many tests! Some study and prepare themselves while others are clueless. Your ability to open to the "flow of life" because of your belief is admirable. To open to the "unseen world" as you do, allows support and insight to be yours at all times.

The greatest of tests these last few days is too offer another respect in how they choose to live their life. It is a process and game to play this "relationship of life" with others. It clouds the mind of many when fear is chosen. The reality is to know what is the fear that is expected. All need to see the big picture and how all play a part in everything that happens individually daily in life.

These last few days simply were a warning of what is still to come. Where there is no change, no rest, no "reflection on self," then what is to be expected is not a desired outcome. Being open to know to go within, and change is extremely needed in humanity that is full of fear and on overload.

Day 160

Violet, the vastness of the unseen world is magnificent!
What can you share with me this day that I will benefit from?

The light of your love beckons out in the unseen world. It is that which now has opened the "portals of true belief" to all that is and has always been unseen. You, my dear Kali, have journeyed forward to now know the "truth of self." It has been a deep discovery to know, believe, and trust the "unseen world" as you do.

I am thrilled when you can feel the "essence of support" from all that surrounds you. To know and experience the "oneness of life" is a blessing that you have manifested this life experience. In your mind's eye is the vision from the "unseen world" that is true beauty.

Gaia feels your love. The elementals are joyous when you smile with belief during the day, just bringing them to mind. The "rituals of words," incense, and knowing what your truth is, allows the Angels, Archangels, and Masters to gather by you. It is your love for animals and the dreams that are preparing you to "open your heart" in total commitment to them. Love is who you truly are!

Day 161

Violet, what can you tell me about The Seven Sacred Flames, by Aurelia Louise Jones that I have chosen daily?

The support of this "window of wisdom" is from all. We, the "unseen world," work together and embrace your willingness. There is much to release, to remember, and to renew now as the "truth of self." The dragon world, elementals, master, etc., are filled with love and guidance to help your "journey of a deep discovery of self."

Kali, it is a time for beauty and opening the heart to Gaia. There is magic from the elements of life. Earth, Water, Fire, Air, and Spirit applaud your choices. It is your eagerness to do and to be the "truth of self" that has brought you to this day.

The "openness of self" will allow the "expansion of your heart" on this wondrous discovery. It is all about learning to teach. In doing so, you raise your vibration, which in turn will raise humanity's vibration.

The path now will ascend quickly as the "window of your soul" opens to the truth of the Seven Sacred Flames. Practice makes perfect! Consistency is respected. Never deviate from your heart's guidance. The "memory of wisdom" rests within the soul and the "heart of self." Follow as you do, and stay on your path, for it is your passion. You now have the platform to do so.

Day 162

Violet, help me to understand what is now expected of me and the connection to the unseen world?

Our connection is the belief of your soul to show you the "truth of life." There is a vast support team for all. It is this that is expected of you now to share. You believe, so a teaching of this journey can now be shared with all of humanity. This is your purpose and connection to all that has been developing.

Kali, yesterday you survived pain, despair, fears, and abuse because of your connection to your Totem Spirit Animals. All are capable as you have been to develop the "force of self," knowing of the support and guidance that is available. Many humans are connected to animals, whether they be dogs, cats, horses, chickens, cows, pigs, birds, etc.

Simply, all they need to do is embrace this connection today. Look up the gifts and power of an animal you are drawn to. Communicate with them daily. Purchase objects that you desire to bring their symbol into the life you live.

All Animal Spirit Guides want to be acknowledged and loved by humans. It is a belief in us that fuels our being as a "Spirit Guide" for a human, whether it be a dog or cat, unicorn, or dragon. We wait for acknowledgment!

Day 163

Violet, how do you like this new space I chose to write in?

The simplicity of this place allows you vision of Mother Gaia and the "flow of life." The "sacred space" in life is wherever the elements can be brought in. Humans hide in their homes, all closed up and locked in. It benefits you to start your day with the beauty of all that you can focus on. Be open to the elements of life that surround you outside.

Kali, your sacredness is in all the "rituals of your existence." I feel there is an "inner sacred part of self" that needs to welcome the "sight of life" that abounds right outside. The "energy of life" is life. It is the basic belief to love your life. Many fear to enjoy out of guilt. This is not true.

It is the moment to open to the world of Spirit and belief in the "unseen world." Support waits to be of service. Many are jumping for joy that a book, this book is in the making. Love is a choice for all to choose daily. Many refused because of the comfort of their misery they cling to daily.

What if they awakened to the joy of the possibilities if they believed in a Totem Animal Spirit Guides, Dragons, Unicorns, or other Elementals instead? To open to joy, like a child of wonder for all that is possible. Sometimes, a look into the impossible creates the "magic of life" to unfold.

Day 164

Violet, Thank you for helping me when I reach out to you. I appreciate how protected I feel. Do I need to know anything that I am not getting now?

It is a journey of this "inner knowing" that is being grasped by you. I protect you because of the path you are on that will help many. There is always a reason for all that happens in life. Many act surprised, angry, and negative when they use their power to harm themselves or another.

The choices you have made, Kali, empowers the path you designed. Stay focused on your dreams, and all that you desire to manifest for change is upon you quickly. Life is filled with "wonder and magic" for those who believe. Your belief is fueled from that which you love to do daily. Continue doing all that fills your "well of wisdom" to develop.

The journey will only get better the more you discover and accept as alternative, but true. Much support and protection come to you because of the love that overflows from the light of your being for humanity.

Day 165

Violet, Do you have a message for me today?

Kali, this day I share a "gift of insight" that I am aware of all that you are now processing. Your desire and belief to "be of service for humanity" is a blessing for all. There will be a time of despair that you will be guided through. Once all is well on the front of your human life, the magic you desire will manifest. As the days now change, get outside every day to connect to the elementals that wait to welcome you daily.

Life is truly about joining with the seen and the unseen. Kali, it is time for your life to be all that you desire it to be from now on. Do as you would for another as you do for yourself. Being open to our partnership is a teaching that will bring many to learn from you.

They will require knowing how you manifested a Dragon Spirit Guide into your life? How did you know I was protecting you even when you were unaware of my connecting to you? It is this book that will be a map to put you on the map. The "magical, mystical, mystery of life" is in the "power of words and one's belief."

Day 166

Violet, I believe I need help at this time with all that is being expected of me! Can you help me?

There is always guidance available for you. There is never a challenge that will not benefit you personally in the end. Help is what you desire now, Kali? "Ask, and it will be given." The "unseen world" of life only needs questions, a thought, or belief from all of humanity, and help appears. Sometimes the answer rests within for many to embrace.

In your case, all that you have manifested is a bit challenging but very powerful to adhere to learning. Know that all you manifested has been supported, filled with insight for you as well as clarity. There is no fear from you as you journey your path with an "open-heart and love." Let not others tell you what to do or what to expect. "All is in Divine timing."

Your patience in life is a great tool. Stay patient for now. Life and the "Creator of Source Energy" move in a magical way. The path is set. The journey has begun. Stay focused and listen to the information and all the guidance you receive from within now.

Day 167

Violet, the days fly by, and I wonder about the wholeness within, as I am now. Can you explain this feeling within I am aware of?

The human you are has an ego, and it is this that has changed now. The "Spirit of Self" is that which has become embraced. The wholeness can be the joining of both, which are no longer separated. There is no more split or duality present for you, Kali, at this time. This is a teaching to share with others on your journey.

Many feed the ego, and it is that which is necessary in life to separate the self to live in the world of duality. It can be embraced and fed love, not fear, to enjoy the journey of life that one desires. The "manifestations of the soul" are to choose another way eventually. The "energy of life" is the emotions of the ego that needs to know. The soul knows, and there is no chaos or drama.

The wholeness of your experience this lifetime is the joy you possess daily in all that you fill your days with. To be what humans call Spiritual is a joke. All are of Spirit. All are Spiritual. When one chooses to open the door to their experience in Spirituality, the true "journey of life" begins. Where there is a belief in "Sacred Divine Life," one chooses love. One ignites the "Spirituality of body, and mind with their soul."

Day 168

Violet, yesterday was eye-opening and very powerful for me. Did I choose well?

It is a process of human belief to journey in fear and pain. The drama is created in life individually by all. The spiraling out of control to abuse another is dangerous. Karma is the choice in the moment of one's reaction, belief, action, and harm toward self or another.

It seems fear is mostly chosen because of a belief that another is more dangerous and will inflict more pain. However, humans manifest their fear and pain daily by how they choose to live. No one seems to stop, reflect, and try to choose another way. Where there is "love for self," one's children and others, that is the choice needed.

Love is all there is. Anything else is not worthy of choosing. Kali, your way of belief is expanding daily to know you personally choose for yourself, not for anyone else. As a person that has chosen to "be of service," you did well yesterday.

The "essence of life" is the "beam of light and love" that many desire to choose, but instead, fear appears. Life is this "discovery of self" that enhances a knowing that, *"free will"* allows all to benefit from how they choose daily.

Day 169

Violet, I believe there is a flickering light that I witness spinning when I close my eyes. What is this?

Kali, you are aware that it is purple and white as it spins and flickers? The dedication you possess to mankind is being served by the "unseen world of all beings." The opening to all your "inner wisdom" is developing to the depths of many lifetimes. All that you are today is because of the "lessons of wisdom" you appreciated. This is definitely a gift that will be yours to claim.

The third eye is developing a sign now to welcome you forward on your path. The teachings will be many that you shall share. Remember, you desire to do all that you do daily. The joy of your life creates happiness when you allow yourself space that is sacred and time to appreciate all the abundance you witness.

Gratitude, Love, Light, and Forgiveness are powerful tools to use daily as you do. There is a change developing within now. Can you feel it, Kali? Embrace it tenderly for change is expected in human life, and most develop a fear of change. Knowing there is a deeper "purpose in life" serves you well. Open your heart, mind, and soul for all that will change your life, as you know it now.

Day 170

Dearest Violet, what is now going on with my morning download today?

It is a "portal to be and do" all that you are being led to experience. Kali, the "discovery of self," never ends. The layers are many to dig into. There is that which you believe that others do not. This is the teaching to be shared. Look within Self for the answers.

Knowing of the "unseen world" as you believe will benefit many. This day's download can be a blueprint for the "path of belief" you discovered in sharing information. Trust, and you shall receive. Know that you know because you exemplify a true student of life.

To laugh and love the days you are experiencing is to fill with joy and happiness. We, the "unseen world," fill with joy and happiness, as well. The "path of expansion" has many twists and turns.

Walk proudly on your path, for it is unique to you. Do your beliefs and share all you have learned! Play, enjoy, and definitely have fun in the process. There is no need not to.

Humanity will benefit most from the "light of your love" that you beam out for them to embrace now.

Day 171

Dearest Violet, what information can you share with me around this life I have manifested?

Your life is filled with purpose and passion now. It is the manifestation of your "soul's desires." To teach and share information is natural. This day, the fears of yesterday have been erased. There is an "openness of joy" that fills your body, mind, and soul to fulfill your dreams.

Kali, the memory of your Totem Animal Spirit Guides will always be of your journey. Today, you smile at yourself and say, *"I communicate with a Dragon named Violet!"* Yes, you do, and it is wonderful to do so. An "open mind of belief" is the "call of your soul" to share this information.

Your beliefs are different for many to understand. Then there will be the ones who know and believe as you do in the truth of the "unseen world" as it is a fact of life. The mystery is to wander away from the normal beliefs many have been taught. Take a look with wonder, as a child would in the "fairy tales of life," as an existence that is pure delight. We are true, as beings of the "unseen world," waiting to be recognized by all of humanity.

Day 172

Violet, Thank you for sharing information about the unseen world last night. What are the benefits I can take from this?

The "unseen world" is abundant as you have been, witness to. The benefit is in this teaching, and a belief in the world that definitely exists but yet is unseen. Is this where the disbelief stems from, you need to address. Many pray and believe in a God, Creator, Divine Intelligence, which has never been seen. There are prayers to Angels, Archangels, Saints, and Ascended Masters, as well, and yet they are unseen too. Why, then, do humans not believe in the elemental, dragons, unicorns, crystal skulls, and others that are alive but unseen?

In recent years, "Energy healing" has been offered to balance the unseen Chakras within the body, and has become popular. Affirmations, Intentions, Chanting, and Song are used to change a human for the better to the "unseen world" of who, is the question.

It seems, Kali, that now is the time to join together, the "belief of seen and unseen" as the "magical, mystical, mystery of life" as an energy that is extremely powerful. Do you see what the benefits shall be when this is taught to the nonbelievers?

Day 173

Violet, I am delighted to discover a new tool within, as the "diamond heart of love!" Did you have anything to do with this gift I received?

The path of your "discovery of self" has been witnessed by many from the "unseen world." This gift is a tool as you have experienced but never connected to. "Divine timing" is essential at all times. Kali, it is your consistency, focus, belief, and rituals that have now manifested this gift for you to add into your life. It is "within the self" that all wisdom and gifts rest. When the time is appropriate, these gifts will all be revealed.

Love is the essence of opening the mind so that the body reflects the soul's desires. It is a passion of purpose that all possess to claim as their own. Many do not stay consistent with their desires. The desire drifts away like a forgotten dream that is not real.

The "ritual of life" is to stay focused on all that one desires. In doing so, dreams do come true. It is all planned but forgotten, simply released until one awakens and manifests their dream with "love of self."

Day 174

Dear Violet, what is your message for me?

Adaptability is that which is a powerful tool for you to adhere to! There is no means of error in your life. Kali, look around at all you do and how your day is processed. It is a choice of yours to travel this journey "connected to Spirit." No one can tell you differently.

As you open to sharing your world, many will join in your travels to learn from you. Loving the life you have chosen to manifest and exist daily in is a treasure. Many are not filled with such passion, purpose, or focus to simply love themselves and what they choose to create. All that you create is noted and filed in the "sourcebook of your existence."

There is much that has been awarded by anyone who releases fear and chooses love. It is the belief that love is superior to anything else. It is this love that," Fuels the soul," and all that is unseen. My world celebrates you as you "unveil" all that this book offers to humanity.

The world is the map of lessons one travels lifetime after lifetime. The "key to the discovery of self" is the spiritual being witnessing their "humanness" and accepting that they are a "superhuman being!"

Day 175

Violet, I am traveling this new path totally open to belief and possibility with trust for the unseen world. How is this happening?

It is not a mystery for me to witness the "path of self" that you have embraced. The "magic of life" for all of humanity is to witness within the mind's eye that there is an "unseen world" that is part of the "mystical journey of life." Many books, songs, and movies have been trying to open the human mind to this belief. To fill with wonder, to pursue a deeper connection, as you have been, witness to know.

Kali, you simply believe because of the joy you needed at times while filled with despair at a young age. The "innocence of a child" harmed by an adult is not acceptable. The unseen gather to allow the child into the "world of magic" through unicorns, dragons, dinosaurs, and faeries, of course.

There is a reason for everything that manifests in life. It is the "unseen world" of Totem Animal Spirit Guides that draw the heart to open as a comfort when there is fear as a child. We delight in offering our services to a child in need. Most of us travel the entire life span alongside the child into adulthood.

This is all that you have been a witness to, and now you believe in the "world of magic."

Day 176

Violet, Do you have a message for me about the ending of this book we are collaborating on?

Kali, you question the ending? There is none! We are on a "discovery of self" for all of humanity.

The exact closure will be seen by you shortly. The word limit and "day" limit have purpose. Trust that you will know exactly when this book's teaching is ready for humanity to enjoy.

The joy of your life is the written word. For many lifetimes, this wasn't permitted, but this lifetime all dreams are manifesting for your soul. The "unseen world" is in full support of all your desires. The amazing choices that you choose with a "beam of light and love" serve you well, Kali.

Begin a re-reading of our collaboration. There are some additions you need to add in that you took out. It did not make sense before now. However, you now understand the process fully. Our book, *A Key to the Unseen World*, is a story for humanity to wonder of their childhood friends and to rediscover the joy in connecting as an adult. The "unseen world" waits to embrace the inner child of the adults who choose to believe again. Within these words rests the "magical, mystical, mystery of human existence as Spiritual beings."

Day 177

Violet, powerful downloads are taking place over my mind. Who do they come from?

The "unseen world" is filled with many guides that willingly are available for service to you. It is that which humans call the "IAM Presence," that is filling your thoughts. The power humans possess is in this connection that is available for all.

The "IAM Presence" is of the "unseen world," Kali, as you are aware. Now that this is available to you, thread quickly on the messages sent to you to manifest that which is for humanity to raise their vibration.

- The "magic of the unseen world" is that we know what humans do not know.
- The mystical part is the "oneness" that connects all.
- While the mystery is that all that is "unseen" across the board is real. The "realm of this magical, mystical, mystery" of all of life creates "unity" and is available for all to embrace.

Humans are powerful beyond what they can ever imagine. Just look at all that has been created in life. The choice has always been to create a life filled with love, joy, happiness, compassion, peace. Or, to create and live a life of fear, hate, anger, abuse, hatred, and misery. What power humans use has been their *"free will"* to choose always.

Day 178

Violet, what words of wisdom can you offer me about these last few days where I was not able to communicate with you?

Kali, your wisdom is known to me, and I am witness to all you choose to accept in life. The fears of another have no effect on you as they did in the past. Your happy place is communication with the "unseen world." Joy is fully yours even when you are not capable of completing your "rituals" daily.

A great example you possess of being capable is of going with the flow. The essence of all you do by choice is powerful. Stay focused, and even when taken out of your surroundings, return with an open heart, as you do.

The "unseen world" always waits for your connection. I am amazed at the insight and clarity you grasp with love and respect in receiving all that you do. There is an inner part of you that has been able to know, listen, act, and manifest now.

Return to all that is filled with passion for you, and all shall be well. "Change is life," and you are always protected for anything that shall be possible in the future. It is to be, and you will blossom with peace and love within for the memories as comfort from the "unseen world."

Day 179

Violet, what can you tell me about all that is happening in my life of change?

Yes, change is quickly coming to the front for you now. Kali, try to understand that the "rituals" of your existence daily and focused with love is the "alchemy of self." It is you personally manifesting all that is called by you, change. There is a "portal" that waits to welcome you into the "realms" of all the "unseen parts of existence." The "mind of self" is an opening now to discover yesterday's wisdom.

The change, of course, is the full understanding of the "magical, mystical, mystery of life" that is true. To discover such a love for this "inner wisdom" shall bless you further on your path. Recall that this is the truth of one's "discovery of self" to know the entire self; body, mind, soul, and spirit.

It is change only because the human aspect of your being does not recall what the soul knows from lifetimes of traveling your specific journey to get you now to this page writing the words channeled to you from your Dragon Spirit Guide. Think about that, Kali!

MYWOLF

Mywolf walked into the woods slowly. He marveled at the beauty of the snow and frost on the trees. His love for the waterfall stemmed from Kali's love as well. The woods were a scared place untouched by the human world of the internet that nourished Kali the most.

His thoughts traveled to the past and how he inspired and guided Kali as a child to the woman she is today with her Totem Animal Spirit Guides.

He hoped her story will awaken humans to be open to all that is possible. To trust that there is a reason for everything that happens in life. The game of life is daily in the tests offered to all to embrace their lessons.

Chapter Twenty-Five
May 1, 2019

Day 180

Violet, what words of inspiration can you enlighten me with?

Kali, I see all! I know all! I am aware of the changes that interrupt the "flow of your life." Your passion in all that you enjoy is powerful to witness. The team you have gathered around yourself from the "unseen world" is joyful. As you celebrate all that fulfills you, they join in right alongside you.

The "transformational attributes" you have been able to acquire is fuel for your soul's expansion. It is a healing to enjoy "being of the light" and staying "within the light." The challenges of human life are many due to the ego-mind of fear.

To know now that you are fearless and journeying, your soul's path is the power of all you can offer. The basis of this power stems between the thoughts, words, and actions that are now your existence.

Joining with a Spirit Guide at any time is the insight offered to you as a deeper form of guidance. You, Kali, are open and ready to travel into the "unseen world" as a way of "being of service." How does that enlighten you this day?

Day 181

Violet, is there anything I need to know about my path?

Kali, the path you have journeyed has led you into the "realm of the unseen." It is this path of "being of service" by all that you do that is powerful. Stress not what gets added unto your plate.

Know there is and will always be a reason for everything. Be open to look into another way. Discern for yourself what you can use.

When love and belief in another is a reason, there can be no reason not to try another way. Life is a journey of steps forward one at a time. Guidance comes in many forms. Be open and accept all that is given. It is love for all alternatives that shine light on the path of passion and purpose.

Close your mind now to yesterday's beliefs and open your heart to learn all that is required in life at this moment for you to help humanity. After all, that is the true reason for being for all that you have studied—to "be of service" to help humanity "raise their vibration." The "unseen world" supports you and has your back, as you say. Believe there are no mistakes, only possibilities that require action.

Day 182

Violet, what can you tell me about Sam, the Male Dragon, that has joined our team of Spirit guides?

Sam is a powerful male energy of protection that travels to those in need of support to be of "service to humanity." It is his power to help protect Mother Gaia from abuse at times. He watches over the "fairy realm" and the faeries of the grass, trees, air, and water. He provides for them the promise of safety in the human world.

He will wait to meet you when "divine timing" agrees it to be so. As I protect you, he protects what you have and love. The "unseen world" knows as the soul knows the journey to be coming, and in joining together, "alchemy" is rewarded.

Many do not trust or believe as you do Kali, and this does harm to the "unseen world's heart of belief." As you further your abilities with sight, all will be shown to your sight, as we see. There is much to discover that is real but "unseen." Know how protected you are because of your trust, belief, and love for all that you express out into the world.

A unique "being of light and love" is a teaching to share when the heart and mind open to the "unseen world" of *"the all that is."*

Day 183

Violet, I feel I messed up the other day by not being firm on what I desired to do! Why did I not insist?

Kali, it is not your nature to be "fierce for self!" In the past, you could for others. There is no need for guilt at this time. Take these emotions and process them as a "truth of a lesson" you desired. Kali, you cannot help one who does not choose to change. It is not your responsibility.

What you seem to do is open your heart to give another free rein over your life. Think about this, as I am aware that you do. Ask if it is an illness that is surfacing, or is it a power that is strong when it comes to being in control.

To go with the "flow of life" is to move forward as a "being of light and love." Is it not a dream of yours to "be of service?" The "unseen world" has your back. I, Violet, have your back and protect you from harm. Do your part by releasing that which is not yours!

The darkness anyone battles is chosen by them to make sense of life that they cannot control. They choose to control and demand they are right. Think about that. No one has the means of being in control of another unless they are given permission to do so, Kali.

It was not that you released your power; your guilt was to an old belief that surfaced as control. You did not mess up; you opened your heart to help another, and then you saw, in the end, it was needed. When you "choose love," Kali, your light beams out and is comfort for another! It matters not that they know where this comfort stems from but that they feel good.

I applaud you for doing the work to travel forward, knowing this truth. "Kali Lunar," you are as unique as your name. You will know when to use this name on writings as "IAM Kali Lunar!"

Day 184

Violet, I saw the image of Sam, as a huge Dragon of true protection for Mother Gaia at your side! Thank you!

Kali, it is time for such sight to now develop. Your gifts are many, but the love you share is your greatest quality. To travel a human existence in belief of the "unseen world" and never feel alone is a "truth of self." I feel your joy at yesterday's "discovery of self." To be such a "beacon of light" for another is powerful.

- The spiritual "essence of self" is pure light.
- The human essence is the "expression of love."

"Love of self," and all one is capable of is an inner connection to the "soul of self." This is the purity of the mind of God. Stand firm in your beliefs for relationships are a practice time to help the majority that struggles with themselves. It is never about another. It is always about the "love of self" that is empowered by the "diamond heart" within.

Pure love is a light, no matter what human it is shone on. Seek no outcome from who you are, as you are. Simply beam out the "light of self with love" in all situations. Be the "Divine Angel" you are…

Day 185

Violet, I feel an inner peace when I call out to you for your protection in situations! Why is this possible?

It is I that comes forward in your field to protect whatever is required. Kali, I see the despair those around you face. I am aware of your desire to help. Sometimes simply trusting that," All is well" can be enough. What is trust but to know that there is a reason for all, even if one cannot see the outcome? To believe is to trust there is "divine timing" in all situations.

This is difficult to grasp for some. However, Kali, you know the truth of these words. Those who you seek miracles for shall be protected and know that," All is well." It is a "journey of discovery" to heal one's karma. The soul knows what is to be. The human does not because of grasping on to fear.

Where there is light vs. dark, then the outcome is always on what the light is in need of. Where there is innocence of a child's wonder, truth is the light to be brightest. Darkness never wins in a situation fueled by the basis and a foundation of love. "Love is light," and innocence is "wonder of openness to expansion."

Day 186

Violet, I feel free of yesterday's thoughts. I am open to any suggestions you have for me.

The mind is powerful, Kali. It is clear that you seek connection and insight daily from the unseen world by all you manifest. It is beautiful to witness the "process of change" you accept now by the "infusion" of hearing and knowing your connections to the "unseen world."

Kali, your life experience is true for your soul. You have connected in totality to the "soul of self" in wholeness. This is a purity that all can manifest with joy. It is as you have witnessed the gathering of balance within the energy of your field. Being open to experience your "truth of self" is guided by the "unseen world." "Dedication to self" is a path many refuse to walk. Yet, it is golden with insight, clarity, and joy for all who do.

There is an openness that you manifested, and now you will be led to all that is possible for you to "be of service" for humanity. Follow your truth, not what another deems it to be. All is a plan to "discover for self" the journey of one's "wholeness." Be a "way-shower" with an open mind and heart. Heal another as you know to do from the "essence of your truth" and feel free as you do now.

Day 187

Violet, can you tell me something about the crazy world I am experiencing lately?

The human being believes in lack across the board for some reason. Fear of life is a deep belief. Now is the time to release the past to move into the present existence of life. The drama is fuel for the mind's ego. The "Spirit world" has no ego. We, like dragons and all the "unseen world," Kali, are "beings of light and love" as you are.

The difficult human belief is to struggle for some reason. The darkness of the mind is an infliction on the need for power and control. There is much that fuels a person toward anger and hate, which comes from within.

Many choose misery as the only way to exist. It is written, "Do no harm." This is simple, but many humans cannot grasp they must begin by doing no harm to self. It is a known belief in the realm of humanity to harm self, as well as another. This is not acceptable.

Kali, looked around the world of life today and was witness to all the harm supposedly loved ones inflict on one another. It is a crazy world to choose in such a way. To actually believe one benefits from harming anyone ever is not true.

Day 188

OMG Violet, what happened yesterday? My entire energy field crashed!

The emotions that filled your heart and mind overwhelmed your field. Kali, all that you do for self is your journey. You cannot do it for another. All must find their way. You are a true example of change, growth, self-love, and a positive outlook.

Think of the moments where you let others fend for themselves and their choices. Karma is powerful. Hate, anger, and jealousy are powerful. What one extends outward, one will receive eventually. Sometimes you cannot choose how to be supportive, and the emotions overwhelm your field. Emotions are "energy," as well, and trying to comprehend another's choices in life is not your responsibility.

You do best to experience other's choices from the outside. It is theirs, not yours. If there is harm, bless them, pray for them, but never judge them. Be open-minded that, as you know, there is a reason for everything in life. Whether it be harm, hate, or jealousy, there is a purpose. Where there be love, joy, or happiness, there is a purpose. Know all have *"free will"* to choose how they want to experience life.

Day 189

Violet, I have called on you, and I feel blessed for your insight.
What message do you have this day?

The path has been winding and up and down at times. Some moments, there have been blocks by self. Kali, your "discovery of self" is on point. You are powerful. Now design the plan you desire to manifest. Be true to all you need to help yourself, as well as others. Opening you're teaching, and wisdom to reach more has arrived.

Knowing you are not ever alone and have "Spirit Energy" to call on makes your choices now with clarity. You do have control over how you desire to manifest a life by teaching and sharing information. Stop now to cultivate the ideals you need to set and follow what inspires your "journey of self" as the discovery for all you require.

The "unseen world" is ready for you. Ask yourself if you are ready for the future travels into the unseen world. Begin this journey by setting time to journey with the Spirit totem animals of yesterday. Call on them and receive your answers. "To ask is to receive!" Step back from human life and concentrate totally now on the "life of Spirit" and all that is "unseen" to reach the many who are in need of your healing.

Day 190

Violet, what words of comfort and insight do you have for me this day?

Kali, it is time to immerse yourself in the editing of our journey. To drift away from all that has been offered will be a gift for the ego power. The path has been traveled, and the journey now needs to begin. We, as a team, have embraced our worlds with a teaching that is true.

You are aware of the benefits received personally from the "unseen world." The "peeling away of self" that does not "reflect your truth" can be felt as an emptiness within self, a drain of one's "energy." However, it is also a wakeup call to live the "truth of self."

The human self is complicated as it struggles with the chaos of humanness. Balance is required to travel the path that has been designed for you with your permission. Clarity and insight from the unseen world are always provided. It is your responsibility to become aware and choose wisely. There are no mistakes. Take the lessons, move forward, and follow your heart. Hear your soul's call.

Day 191

Violet, difficult times create fear and abuse, as well as harm in humans. Why?

It is the exact moment, the very second that one chooses to react that manifests their emotions.

"Emotions are energy." This "energy" flows up the chakras of the body. One needs to ask; how do I choose to react emotionally? After years of emotional outbursts of fear, guilt, and shame, the body gets affected.

Kali, humans have *"free will"* to choose every moment of the day how they believe. Where there are difficult times of fear and abuse, the harm is to the self, as well as others. There need be no harm if one chooses another way. Where one chooses compassion with love and settles within the heart a song of peace for self or another, that is the outcome to be.

There is a plan. There are lessons that all choose to experience. Where there is criticism or judgment, there is fear. Love is an essence of being that is fueled by connecting to any part that one chooses from the "unseen world." Whether it be through prayer, meditation, or a walk in Mother Gaia, move the choice to how you feel with picking from the variety available from the "unseen world."

Day 192

Violet, I ache! What is going on?

Kali, the tangled web of pain has gripped you. There is no need to speak if the ones you speak to, are deaf to your words. Staying "true to Spirit, Light and Love" is balancing the body and mind with the "soul of self." Being human is not easy. It may be time to detach from the drama of others if you get affected, and they do not.

The "unseen world" has your back, and the purity of your journey is to be grounded in your "truth." Humans play the same record over and over again. In reality, it is a choice, is it not? To now open yourself to doing all you are passionate about takes focus and action. You have tried to please too many. It is time to please Kali. Make choices that serve you.

There is a way for you to journey and find the answers you desire. Begin there, for we in the "unseen world," wait to communicate with you. Open your toolbox to us, and we will be at your side daily. Be "true to self." Know and honor, there is a reason for all in the human life experience. The soul knows all.

Day 193

Violet, what guidance do you have for me?

Kali, the day has finally arrived for you to shed your light for others. There is tremendous change approaching. The end result is "God's Will" in all situations, where there is light, love, innocence, and a need for direction. All is possible with love.

The strength and focus now is to breathe in the moments of "inner peace." "All is well" is a mantra of truth and trust. The thoughts of self-fuel your actions and words, be gentle with all. Many of the "unseen world" support your journey. As you call out to them, they arrive. As your Dragon Spirit Guide, I fire up your spine to its fullest power and strength.

Kali, you can do all that is coming and approaching as change, chaos, and challenge. All will settle down to be a life of fulfillment. The plan has been incorporated by those who can no longer exist in fear. This is the healing and process in the human aspect of life. The soul knows what is needed, and when you connect to all that is "unseen" with love and wonder, "miracles" are than manifested. All in a "divine time."

Day 194

Violet, what message do you have for me today?

Kali, listen to your inner guidance, and stay focused on your desires. It is the "unseen world" that encourages you. Many are aware of the chaos and drama that has manifested. Time is the gift that will shed light on all stories. Remember, life is a school to learn lessons one has chosen.

The "unseen world" is the "Spirit of Essence" in life that graces all who believe and ask for insight. The "dreams of life" for all is love. To be loved, to love, and to love life that one has chosen. No harm will manifest where love opens the heart. Being on this journey now fuels your mind with words to help another.

It is the human concept to exist with drama and chaos to learn another way of being. Does this not make sense to you? The simplicity of life is to make a change, choose another way, have trust there is a process, and "open the heart" for all with love.

All humans, as you are, are Spiritual. The "balance in life" is to awaken to one's "spiritual essence" and choose to live a "spiritual life" while in a human body. That is a balance that you are aware of. Stay with Spirit now!

Day 195

Violet, I feel detached from the unseen world lately. Why?

Much has transpired in your life at this time. Your thoughts are scattered as your emotions are taking over. We have not detached from you in any way.

If and when you call on us, we are there to comfort and protect. The signs have been given. Be open to know you are never alone.

The drama of human creation is scary, but as you know, Kali all has a reason. Your power is love that you offer unconditionally. It is your belief that you desire to heal others. Be open to the fact that fear stops others from healing. You must always allow *"free will"* to be the plan. This is humanity's given right from the Creator.

It is a time of stress for sure, and chaos fuels many you love at this time. Take the moments you are given to return to your passions because there will be times of interruptions for some days. When you can center yourself, be with Mother Gaia, as much as possible. We would never ever, as beings of the "unseen realm," detach from you. Stay open to hear us.

Day 196

Violet, I am thrilled to receive clarity now. How does this happen so quickly?

Kali, the tools of your abilities are gathered in "light and love." Silence, at times, allows you to know the "power of insight." Clarity comes when the hour is early, and the day has not begun. It is these moments that offer you a look within and find the wisdom needed. Know, I know what you can benefit from when you open to love.

It is not simple to choose love as a human. Yet, it is the "essence of your soul." Connection to your soul is a teaching. A "mastery of inner healing!" Kali, belief in all that you receive as clarity is due to this connection. To believe is to connect. One needs to believe in "soul work" as a means to "discovery of self." The soul knows. The soul is love. The soul is waiting for a connection.

The essence of being a human is to discover one's soul, and in doing so, the self becomes whole. You have awakened this day to this moment by the actions you strive for, to "be of service" to humanity. Yes, Kali, all you ache to be and do, your soul is aware of.

Day 197

Violet, I feel we are coming to the end of the text for this, our book, A Key to the Unseen World... Is this true?

Kali, the book will be completed and ready for editing to be published. You know the process, although this is not the end of our communication in the future together. You can continue with me as your Dragon Spirit Guide through your thoughts, dreams, or channeling. This will be a choice to make.

When the book gets published, you will teach the magnificence of knowing the "unseen world" waits to help humanity. All that is needed is belief and acceptance to hear and listen to the guidance given. Many ask and receive answers, but choose to not follow through.

Becoming aware of the benefits of oneness across the board is part of the process of remembering self. All need to open the mind, heart, and soul of remembering. It is a requirement to know who one is. It will allow manifestations of one's dreams. The human of today needs to release all that is not true for them. Then to remember what is, to "renew their journey."

MYWOLF

Slowly, Mywolf stretched out his paws as he thought of Kali and how she has adapted to this channeling process. First with him, and now with Violet! He knew the difficulty humans manifest from fear of not knowing. He discovered a long time ago that humans needed to trust that they are powerful when it comes to manifesting their life experience. Yet, he has witnessed their lack of power by their choices daily.

Separation and fear rule most humans daily because of the programming they have received.

Mywolf knew that Kali had never been programmed to believe what others did but instead went within for her answers.

Chapter Twenty-Six
June 1, 2019

Day 198

Violet, please, speak to me of what is to come now?

The journey has led you to this day of reflection and celebration of your life. Choose wisely the "path of self" that you require. The lessons and guides have been many over the years. Kali, an open heart of love filled with belief for the "unseen" is a gift that has been given to you.

There are no mistakes where the "magical, mystical, mystery" of life is embraced. No one can be you. No one can do what you can do. The "discovery of self" is to be true to your passions at all times. Look at where you are at this very moment and congratulate yourself for all that has brought you to this page.

There is always change that allows one to flow in a different way as needed. The life of many has no desire for change, and they become stuck in an existence of despair. Kali, you are an open window of joy and love. Those who are not open as you are, struggle with their demons daily. To heal from the past is to embrace the "soul of self," daily. All are Spirit first, then human. One's wholeness is balancing themselves by choosing Love. Love is Spirit.

Day 199

Violet, what message do you have today?

There is joy in my heart that you welcome me into your existence, Kali. As you are aware of my essence when I fire up your spine, we have now joined whenever you need a *"lil fire"* to get your point across. The sorrow of yesterday you felt was not yours but a release of your past finally. You are unique to know this.

Crazy, wild, out of control is the "Spirit of Self" that you possess. Be true to these actions and smile. It is the knowing that many do not share as you do. It is this not knowing that defines the 3rd-dimensional Spirit/Human compared to those like yourself, that exist as 5th-dimensional Spirit/Humans. All are Spirit and light, but their fears fuel the ego as they cling to their demons.

My message this day is to be you no matter what. Do as you have been doing when it comes to your daily passions. It is your right to be "free," and this can be a teaching of yours. "Freedom" of the past that no longer serves you with affirmation, intentions, and intuition. Stand "free" in your choices always when love is the path chosen no matter what the situation may be. Cling not to others 'lessons that are not yours is a deep clarity.

Day 200

Violet, what are my gifts? This is the question that popped into my mind this morning...

- "Adaptability" is a gift that far exceeds humanity's journey.
- Choosing "silence" at times has also served you well your entire life.
- Offering to "be of service" by sharing with others is a true "path of self."
- To "love all unconditionally" is a powerful path you have manifested well this entire lifetime.
- "Acceptance" of all to let them live their lives and choose for themselves has eased your journey.
- "Soul connection" is a gift of affirmation, intention, and intuition that manifests freedom of the 3rd-dimensional existence.

It is this "freedom of self" that is your major gift to teach.

To be "free" in life as a spiritual being, you have embraced these gifts many times. It is the "journey of discovery" that unfolds for the self when one always goes within for the answers that," fuels the soul."

To know the self of one's soul is a true "discovery of mastery" of the "wholeness of life" as a human. The "Spirit of Self" is the combining of this wholeness finally.

Day 201

Violet, I thank you for communicating with me! What is next for us as Human/Spirit/Dragon?

Consistency, focus, determination, and clarity are now joined together. The guidance of the Spirit/Elemental/Unseen World is for all of humanity. Pay attention to the children who collect dragons, unicorns, angels, dinosaurs, and any "unseen being" at this time. This is the wonder that is unfolding as the "truth for children." The "faeries" are seen by the children of today. The ghosts of past lives are being embraced.

Open the minds of adults by the child is the "magic of truth." The "unseen world" is not a "fairy tale" but a real existence waiting to help humans. All that is required is belief in that which can benefit the living but is unseen.

The fun part of adult life has been collecting totem animals or having certain animals as pets. Many now need to realize this. Pets in your house are Totem Animal Spirit Guides for each one who lives with them.

There are dog people, cat people, horse people, bird people, or fish people because of the power of these animals that is "unseen" but powerful to behold. There is a reason for everything in life, and what you are drawn to have a purpose and reason for existence in life at this time.

Day 202

Violet, I ask for guidance to help those in fear. How do I help another?

Kali, the help to offer is to witness the fear and offer "light and love." It matters not if it is absorbed from them. Fear and anger are deep within the essence of many you love. It cannot be your responsibility to erase what they have individually manifested as their belief.

The battle for many in a human life experience is to fuel the ego before trusting their Creator. All are co-creators but need to connect to this "belief of self." It takes diligence to work on the "mind of self" and "choose love." Many humans fear the unknown. The "unseen world" that waits to offer insight, clarity, and guidance is unknown.

Fear needs to be released as that which is not healthy for one's body, mind, or soul in any form. "Energy" is fueled by one's emotions. If the "energy" is not of love, joy, and happiness on a consistent daily basis, fear is enforced as a choice. The question is, "What does one fear and why?" All are of the "light" as "Spiritual Beings" with no fear, only love. Balance is required to even out one's beliefs to feel better by choosing love.

Day 203

Violet, what is your message for me?

Human life is ruled by the self of ego. It is a human condition to react in a negative, "Get you back" attitude. Of course, Kali, this is of the 3rd-dimensional mentality. Karma is quick as Mother Gaia cleanses herself of toxins and debris. It is to be the same for humans to cleanse as well.

"Light and Love" are power choices of the Soul for all to generate toward. Where the choice is Spirit, love unfolds and opens the journey to joy, happiness, and inner peace. It is time, now, to "choose love," as all are "beings of Light."

Chaos, frustration, abuse, and challenges are not of the "Light." When they appear, a lesson to learn is a given option. Any harm to another consciously is selfish and requires instant karma as a result. Blame—karma. Abuse—karma. Negative thoughts, words, and actions—karma.

It is a choice given to all how they want to live daily. Choose wisely as an example for others that are part of your journey. Human life is the "act of giving and sharing" with Love because of *"free will."* The "unseen world" supports all "acts of Light and Love."

Day 204

Violet, how can I travel at night with you?

Kali, we do travel at night, but it is now erased from your memory at daylight. The nightlife of many humans would frighten them if they remembered these travels. The "unseen world" is a world where many have been witnessed to during the night. There is a reason for this lack of memory at this time.

The mind of humanity can only comprehend so much that is not of the normal vision of life. That is why the mind's eye is opened by books, movies, and music. It is the doings of the "unseen world" to gently ease humans toward another way of belief.

There is a "magic, mystical, mystery" for humans that join in belief with the "unseen world" as a "realm of truth." It takes time to open to a belief of knowing it is possible. The next process is to witness with one's mind and sight the reality of *'the all that is"* real, true, and possible.

We Spirit guides bring protection, comfort, and joy to humans on their journey of "discovery of self" as "Spirit/Human." So many have no sight at all that they are a living, breathing "Spiritual Being" first.

Day 205

Violet, what insight can you share with me about all I am experiencing?

The lessons of life chosen to learn have empowered you to open the "heart of your soul." Kali, your wisdom and "inner insight" is a gem you can offer to the fearful. Your life has not been a breeze to experience. However, where there is love, one learns quickly to embrace a "spiritual path" that, "empowers" one's soul to heal.

The "mastery of life" is to hold space for one another. As the soul is an eternal part of everyone's existence, a healing of one's karma is now possible. Kali, your love for life and the "acts of service" and sharing has brought you to this page. The "unseen world" is part of your day in many forms. The "rituals of life" that you offer fuels us all. We are greatly infused by your choices.

The wonder of life is the belief of one's choices by their thoughts, words, and actions. The superpowers of humanity are simply ignited this way by their choice to choose another way to be as you have succeeded in doing.

Day 206

Violet, can you share with me your message about lessons to learn?

The journey is one of "true light" that becomes a "discovery of the soul of self." There is no other lesson for being but to discover one's "inner self of love." All are light. All are love. The choice of *"free will"* as a test for humanity is to discover that all can choose for oneself.

It is a plan designed in the world of Spirit…the family, friends, and parents that will activate an "inner essence" of one's truth. The veil is thin, and the "unseen world" waits to be welcomed into humanity's "mind of self," as a belief. What is not seen is that of the "Spirit World" between birth and after death! This is a fear that many cling to because it is not believed that there is more to life.

Life is a place to "discover the self" and to live a "life of love" to forgive, accept, and fill with joy for all experiences that are possible for the opening of one's gifts of light. The soul knows all and the "unseen world" as well is witness to the struggles humans enforce upon themselves daily as part of their life experience. To awaken to choose another way of being is a true "discovery of self."

Day 207

Violet, is there anything I need to know from your realm of the unseen?

The beauty of our collaboration is the "silence" within. My realm is silence as we communicate through "telepathy" one to another. It is this that is fueling your journey. Many are clueless of the need for "silence" in their life. "Silence" empowers the "discovery of self," to know, hear and, witness the "mind of self." There is much noise and havoc in the human world that erases the beauty of Mother Gaia.

The blast of "silence" on a daily basis calms the soul. To choose wisely, the words expressed are a "power of self." Mother Gaia offers song and grace of life, but many are extremely busy and lack the desire to awaken to her gifts. Much change is needed by humans to save Gaia and embrace her as a home for all.

In the "unseen world" of the "elementals," especially, all work together to heal Gaia daily. It is a love of peace and joining together in "silence" to heal what humans do. The few that are aware are not enough compared to the many that abuse their home. Kali, "Silence" is a beginning to hear the cry of Gaia's call.

Day 208

Violet, I have a deep inner peace that has settled within. Where is this stemming from?

All that you are passionate about as a "being of light" is your "truth of self." It is an awakening to the discovery of this that is the essence of "inner peace." As you offer your services through the written word, healing, and listening skills, the Universe applauds.

The "unseen world" is capable of many gifts and blessings to the one who is focused and consistent. The term is, "As you heal, All heal." When there is a purpose fueled by love, the "unseen beings" wake up to "be of service," as well.

It is the path one travels that enlightens the journey as a "discovery of truth." Where there is truth, peace is experienced. "Human/Spirit" becomes "whole of self," and the "Spirit of Self" embraces the "Human Temple" as a place to experience lessons and heal karma of the past. Today's karma, as you are aware, Kali, is instantly resolved.

The "energy of life" on Gaia is now that the 5th-dimensional realm beckons all to awaken to the changes needed to become "beings of light and love" to release the 3rd-dimensional realm that is no longer working for many on Gaia.

Day 209

Violet, is there any insight you can share with me today?

Connecting deeply to the "inner wisdom of self" is a "magic existence." All that is wise, love, passion, and filled with joy is supported by the "unseen world." Kali, the human mind is extremely conflicted in all thoughts, words, and actions. The sensitive choices one clings to can be a trigger from a lesson not learned.

To heal the mind stems only from the thought process. If humans believe in their demons and fuel them by the process of choice through daily thoughts, words, and actions, a vicious cycle becomes a reality. To step away from an unhappy pattern that has formed takes diligence, focus, and a deep change of belief.

No one is capable of helping one that refuses to be helped. Where there is fear, guilt, and shame that one feels victim to, they must choose for oneself a change in their process. The "unseen world" is full of helpers from the many realms; Angel, Spirit, Elemental, and Animal. To ask for guidance, insight, and clarity is a step that opens the necessary realm to "be of service." But one must ask for help!

Day 210

Violet, I felt you at my side, comforting me last night. Is this a truth?

Kali, your awareness, insight, and ability to know all is your truth. As the "unseen world" supports, protects, and inspires you, we are always aware of your needs. There is an army that waits to "be of service" for you as well as any that asks for help.

The human realm is toxic and filled with chaos by human's own choice. The cleansing of Mother Gaia continues because change is required. Less of everything is desired as a healing for all. Refuse to accumulate waste in stuff that is not helping Mother Gaia.

Humans need to awaken to a belief in living with less, to donate to the needy, and to respectfully live a life of focus. To focus on oneself and to "be of service" to another in need is what is being asked for all of humanity.

The world is literally at everyone's fingertips now with the internet. Purchase less to accumulate less. The "unseen world" is pleading for humanity to open their eyes to the abuse Mother Gaia is experiencing. No one is alone in any way. We know all and support whoever asks for us to help them.

Day 211

Violet, what is your message for me today?

There is joy, love, and light surrounding you at all times. Be aware of the "subtle energies" of all "elementals" that support you daily. I, as your Dragon Spirit Guide, is the "kundalini flame" that travels up your spine in moments of truth. It is a deep belief in the "unseen world" that fulfills your mind now. Sight is to be, as well as anything else you desire. It is definitely a "desire of self" to discover the truth of one's existence.

Many humans fear knowing their truth because of feelings of being unworthy. Let the light in, and the "discovery of self" is finally revealed. As humans learn of the basic belief that all are one and of the light, all heal. The "magical, mystical, mystery" of existence is to awaken to heal and "master the soul of self." There is no hidden agenda, Kali.

It is the simplicity of life to use your energy with love and joy daily. To be of positive and kind thought, word, and action allows love to be the "light of self for others." This is a simple tool to acquire...love is all there is.

Day 212

Violet, I met "Sam the Dragon" yesterday and felt his power and protection. I was guided to look up to the sky and take a picture of the clouds, and there he was! OMG! What does this mean?

Kali, the "elemental realm of Spirit," and the world of Dragons are beckoning to you in many ways. Know you are blessed to feel the "energy," see, and be protected by them. It is an opening to the 5th-dimensional world that is to be part of the change that is required. Opening yourself now to the insight and clarity that is yours is a "truth of acknowledging" that the reality of life is that the "unseen world" is a "realm" that waits to be known by all.

The wave of the trees is a unique truth of acknowledgement for you, Kali. Many live a blind life when it comes to all that is possible by the mere question of asking to know all of life. As many are open to see, truly see the self, the door opens in "divine timing."

No fear or doubt, the more that exists than what is believed is the map to uncover. The "unseen world" of existence as "truth of self," with belief as a simple thought that no one is ever alone on their journey of "discovery of self."

Day 213

Violet, there is so much drama in life! Is it all created by the ego?

Kali, the fear of the ego is powerful. Humans fear love to begin with. Fear the eyes of another on them! Fear their own thoughts, and if they are worthy. Many humans carry the drama in life of another. In doing so, they do not realize it is not of their own making, and fear settles in. The greatest of fears is to be jealous and let another's choices fill your mind with disbelief of self.

The "unseen world" watches all that humans choose as if they are under a spell. It is now that the spell needs to be broken. Look within, connect to the "truth of self," and "choose to love." Of course, the first one to love is the self, to "open the heart" to love all. As one heals, all heal. To be open-hearted is to love, period, in all situations, not to pick and choose, but to love no matter what.

The "discovery of self" is the greatest lesson to adhere to and learn. Humans are meant to be free of social belief and instead choose their own belief in life as a "spiritual being" now.

Day 214

Violet, can you guide me further on the path of true spiritual light at all times?

The "path of spiritual light" as a human now is one of truth, love, and harmony. To have an open "heart of love" to share is a truth, and one experiences harmony. There is no need to guide you on something that has been a "mastery of self." Kali, there is either light or dark. You are a Light.

So many choose harm as their choice that they dim their "Light." Eventually, the "aura of self" becomes dark where there is negativity, jealousy, lies, anger, or hate. Many are not able to stop themselves, and they stay on a path of 3rd-dimensional mentality.

Some who are leaning toward the "Light" struggle with the ego to be seen, to be heard, but that is the ego's need, and then they move on back to the "Light of Self." "Light or dark is a belief," a "way of being." Many show you exactly who they are, thinking you do not see the dark of self, as well. Fools are what they are. Whatever harm is given, also does harm to the self, as well. Stay true to your light.

Day 215

Violet, what message do you have for me?

Kali, you are opening more and more daily to the "power of belief." The "unseen world" applauds you. The clarity and insight that you are witness to now is a full "empowerment of self." I see you enjoy all that you do for self and another. "Opening your heart" to "be of service" is a choice many do not grasp.

As you are aware, many are clueless about their own power when it deals with how they emotionally think and speak. Where there is anger, pain resides in the body. It is an action that fuels the ego of self. It is not of love. This is a teaching in itself. "Choose love!" "Send love!" "Express love!" "Offer love!"

Love is the natural essence of all humans born of "light and love." To awaken to know this is a powerful moment for all. To observe, listen, and offer clarity and love to another is a "gift of service" as well as a "gift of love."

Humans manifest everything they do not want and fill with fear. "Energy is energy" across the "path of life," Kali, in all forms, but the power resides within all human thought, word, and action.

Day 216

Violet, I am honored to have communication with you and the Spirit World. Is there anything that is required of me now?

Kali, the "path of self" requires focus, consistency, and due diligence for all to expand. To raise one's consciousness is a "journey of change." Staying "true to self" in all chaos enlightens your input daily when you can. It is the greatest of tools to spend outside with the elements. As you are aware and with the weather permitting, be open to her call.

When she beckons, answer, and spend time with her. It is the essence of Gaia's energy that grounds one to her strength. The aspect of life is balance, and the tool is to love the life you are living.

Humans choose their lessons, and then they complain about them. This is an awareness you possess. Begin to sit with Mother Gaia when you can. The warmth will do you tremendous good on your path. Take "time for self, and soul nourishment" from all the elements that are available.

MYWOLF

This month is Kali's birthday month and Mywolf wished her the best in the coming year as she prepares to share her story of him, Violet, and the unseen world of Totem Animal Spirit Guides. May the truth of life and the power humans possess be revealed now by calling on the elemental unseen world...

Mywolf knows that Kali is aware that everything means something and that there is a reason for all of life. Mywolf imagines her in his mind's eye sitting by the waterfall and meditating as she had done so many times.

His heart opens wide for all that she has experienced and desires to share now with humanity.

Change is definitely required by the human race in the future. How they think, speak and act is their 'free will' to choose wisely now.

Chapter Twenty-Seven
July 1, 2019

Day 217

Violet, I have called on you, and I am grateful for our connection these last three days! Empower me with your wisdom, please!

Well, let me see what has transpired that I feel has blessed you most.

- The "elementals of life" are excited for the time you spent with them lately.
- The "open heart of your soul" basked in the warmth of Mother Gaia's sun.
- The calm flow of the water cleansed you as well.
- There is always the choice of being grounded in your life by walking without shoes and being outside.
- Time to renew, release, and refresh oneself is only possible by being outside.

You, my dear Kali, breathed in three days of her "magic and the mystical of life" shall unfold Gaia's "mysteries" for you. Never imagine that time for the self is not needed even with others around you. Doing what you need to process the human chaos of others will definitely be helpful to your journey. It is this "path of service" you are on that benefits most with boundaries. Stay focused on your needs now and many avenues will be open for you to explore.

Day 218

Violet, help me to move forward on this path I have been led to travel!

Kali, you are a "light being" from many different life experiences. The opening of your beliefs to be totally alternative is a sign that you have journeyed forward. There is no end to the journey. There are only lessons to be learned. Choices you need to take to "travel your path" with an "open heart."

What do you desire for you? This is the question you can only answer! Reflect on what no longer serves you to move forward at a pace that will fulfill your desires. This time is a time to plan, reflect, learn, and enjoy life as it is now.

The future waits with open arms for change, growth, and expansion of self. All is of "energy" and opening to others "energy" is a lesson in love and acceptance. Any annoyance that drains you needs to be healed and released. Do not take on beliefs that do not serve you. Be true to all that you are filled with passion for. Live and share your "light" through your purpose now.

Day 219

Violet, at times, do I spend the majority of my day in the 5th dimension of thought?

It seems you travel back and forth at times due to society that still is of the 3rd dimensional mentality. The journey is most difficult when many are not open to "change of belief." The "mind of self" knows until the 3rd-dimensional people step forward as knowing what they know but are not open to change.

Kali, this is why your time and rituals are a daily requirement now. Being accepting of how others choose to stay in the 3rd dimensional mindset is a lesson to acquire and learn. *"Free will"* as the experiment in life allows all to choose for the self, their thoughts, words, and actions.

The chaos in life is due to those who stay rooted in fear, negativity, and no trust in a higher source. It matters not; that is why the option is to allow humans to decide for themselves.

The 5th-dimensional mindset has no fear and walks a "path of love." The basis of belief is, we are all "One" with no separation. The joy in life is to "be of service" and to share with others.

Gratitude is the essence of believing there is a reason for all in life. Trusting in a "higher divine intelligence" is the world of the 5th dimension that you travel to daily but then get yanked back into the mindset of those who choose to stay put in negativity, fear, and worry.

Day 220

Violet, I hope it was allowed for me to lend you out to another that needs your protection?

I am your Dragon Spirit Guide at the service for you and yours. Where there is love in your heart to be shared through prayer, energy, words, or offering of my services, I am ready to be of service. It is a major shift in your mind, Kali, to be so open now. Fearless is the word that comes to mind.

- Love is always the glue in all relationships.
- Love is life!
- Love is a belief!
- Love is the essence of sharing!

May those you share your life with be blessed to know you and believe in the "power of the self!" It is always a teaching to observe in another's "strength of belief." To do as one believes is key to inner power, and this is the path of a true spiritual gifted person.

Being open to the "unseen world" is an offering to another when shared as a gift you possess. Those who are ready to believe and change will come forward and learn all you can teach. There is no other way to learn but by example and the sharing of information as a "way of believing," there is a reason for all in life.

Day 221

Violet, what can you tell me about gratitude and having you as my Spirit Guide?

Let me begin with the "journey of self," and all that has been your true experience. Kali, you fed your soul with books and animals with a deep love of Mother Nature. Mywolf aided you through the journey with Spirit Guides in different forms. This is the look within that ignites connection.

All humans have this ability but refuse to open to it. All are led by what the "soul of self" knows is needed. I appeared when you needed me, and I have summoned Sam as a Dragon Spirit Guide as well, to "be of service" to you. Never forget your power, and beliefs are true for you.

When it comes to gratitude, many refuse to look and see the life journey as one that exists as one manifests. To be grateful for one's choices and experience, especially with the chosen family and friends, is the true process of being grateful.

In reflection, you can renew the journey and receive a healing by being open to the beliefs of gratitude for all of life's experiences. There is no other choice but to be grateful, especially if your life is abundant and fulfilled. "Loving the self" leads one to "love their life journey."

Day 222

Violet, I have begun the task of editing our book as I have been guided to do. Is this the plan now, to be ready to send it out?

It is to be our journey together to release our collaboration and channelings out to the world. A source of delight for me is your willingness to do so. Your bravery, Kali, is magnificent to witness. The path has evolved into a deep belief, a "knowing of the self" through "discovery of connection." There are many ways to connect to the "soul of self."

- The path of Mother Gaia
- Totem Animal Spirit Guides
- Belief in the unseen world as a journey to more in life

The "magic map of life" is many paths, but the destination is the journey. What comes from meditation, prayer, and journaling is an opening of "self-discovery." To gaze at the moon and acknowledge the essence of its power in life. The alternatives to life are everlasting. The elemental realm of the "unseen" is also everlasting. The "soul of self," as well, knows all. What is important is belief, love, and adaptability that the "unseen world" is real, powerful, and ready to help all!

MYWOLF

Mywolf was extremely proud of the journey Kali has traveled with the elementals of life as her guides. It is a deep honor for him to have been her main Totem Animal Spirit guide for so many lifetimes. If only humans would open their minds to the magical, mystical mysteries of life, how glorious their lives would be, he thought.

The essence of truth for Mywolf was that in the unseen world time is not a question. All simply is, as it should be.

Mywolf was aware that Kali discovered the belief of "Service of self" and "Service of others" as a choice that allowed negative or positive thoughts, words, and actions.

The human belief has always been centered on "free will" as an experiment to choose for the self. However, it was imagined from the teachings of "Jesus the Christ" that humans would awaken to love one another and Do No Harm. Instead, "Service of self" became prominent from dark forces on Earth. Few were able to open their hearts or their minds to all humans, animals, plants, and especially the planet. Abuse in any form stems from "Service of self."

With the guidance of Mywolf and Violet, Kali knows now is the time to switch over to "Service to others" as a way to help the planet and all of humanity to raise their vibration. It has been a "power call" for the dark negative forces to control, but it is no longer an option.

The world has to change by making different choices toward love, compassion, joy, and happiness because all are "One!"

In Conclusion...

I am Kali Lunar, and I began this story while I was traveling "Into the Woods" to sit and meditate at my waterfall.

Mywolf appeared and spoke to me about choosing another way of being. He took me into the world of my existence and the many Totem Spirit Animal Guides that comforted me through abuse, abandonment, fear, guilt, and shame growing up.

However, during those times, I was never aware that there was a purpose. Today, I know that there is a reason for everything and everyone that travels in life alongside us. We are all gifted with a passion and purpose to discover.

The truth is that originally, I was calling this book "Into the Woods: A Discovery of Self!"

In 2018, I met Violet and was given a new name for our story, "A Key to the Unseen World." I have been in collaboration with Violet, my Dragon Spirit Guide in Part Two of this story, as you have read.

Every morning, we would communicate. I would light a candle to clear and raise the vibration of the room and to communicate with the "unseen realm." *(In doing so, I also partnered with Earl of the Sidhe, but that is another story to be told in the future.)* I would take time to go into my Akashic Records, as well, periodically.

Daily, I begin my day by meditating, praying, and channeling. In the past, it was taking a pen to paper in my journal. Today, "My Belief" is that," Life is Sacred, I am Sacred," and the "Temple of my Home is Sacred."

Respect for my life as it is today has grown by the tools I have encapsulated into my existence consistently. During my collaboration with Violet, I was introduced to a powerful, huge Dragon named Sam, as well. He is a protector of the woods that I travel to and where this story originated from with Mywolf.

The many days I have taken pen to paper has been the truth of my journey in life. IAM ready to receive! IAM fearless! IAM filled with the wonder of a child that anything is possible. Violet introduced me to Claire a Healing Unicorn in 2019 because at this time humanity is required to open their hearts and minds to the help that is possible for Peace on Earth. All we as humans are required to do is to ask for help in all situations where there is fear, guilt, and, shame. It is our Dragons, Unicorns, and Totem Animal Spirit guides that wait to be called on.

I embraced the world of Humanity, Angels and Elementals with Love! For in my heart IAM a witness to the truth of life…

In reading this story, the "magical, mystical, mystery of life" will now unfold for you, as well. The "Sacred Words" that I have shared with you will empower your thoughts, words, actions, emotions, and intentions as they are coded with the energy of transformation…

MYWOLF

Mywolf met with Violet and discussed how fast Kali embraced their teachings.
Mywolf was the first to travel into her human brain to heal her despair and fears, and to be known. Kali was a terrified child at one time with many fears but the Totem Animal Spirit Guides helped her to heal. It was years of Mywolf guiding her and inspiring her towards change that he had been summoned to bring in all her Totem Animal Spirit Guides, as well.

The plan was to introduce her to Violet, her own Dragon Spirit Guide now because of the energy of Gaia that needed help to raise humanity's vibration. The Collective Council of "the all that is," had met and decided that Violet would be accepted or not. It was one thing to have a stuffed monkey or pig or other symbols of animals as a Guide, but a Dragon?
Kali went with an open heart and mind into their collaboration.

The Universe got on board the plan and Unicorns, Dragons, and Crystal Skulls became injected into the minds of children again. In the past, they were stated as faery tales. Today, the children were wiser and in need of helping their parents and accepted the energy of them as magical. Life was in need of change and it is with the unseen world that it will be possible Mywolf and Violet agreed.

This night... Mywolf and Violet entered the mind of Kali and she was surrounded by them and all her Totem Animal Spirit Guides once again. Her energy expanded as she traveled to her home planet of Lyra and was honored as a human to be accepting of all that she has been witness to with Mywolf and Violet. Horse galloped in as the white stallion of Freedom of her soul for Kali that she was honored by all that she accepted with love.

Now that the story was told, that will change the world as the plan for the unseen world to manifest as real in the minds of adults as they reflect back on their childhood and the support they too received from a Totem Animal Spirit guide. Mywolf knew the power of the mind and that the word is the law.

A **Key** to the Unseen World, I now offer to you… BELIEVE!

Love, Wisdom, and Power, I AM Kali Lunar.

CPSIA information can be obtained
at www.ICGtesting.com
Printed in the USA
BVHW051235110423
662129BV00007B/534